How to Grow Food

How to Grow Food

Your crop-by-crop guide to growing, cooking & preserving

HUW RICHARDS & SAM COOPER
THE *SUNDAY TIMES* BESTSELLERS

Contents

Introduction	06
Growing Essentials	08
Techniques for Growing	010
Growing in Beds & Containers	012
Making Your Own Compost	014
The Self-Sufficiency Formula	016
Polyculture	018
Kitchen Staples	022
Kitchen Techniques	024

ROOT VEGETABLES — 030
Potato	032
Carrot	038
Parsnip	042
Swede	044
Beetroot	046
Radish	050
Turnip	052
Celery	054
Celeriac	056
Fennel	058

FRUITING VEGETABLES — 060
Tomato	062
Pepper	068
Aubergine	072
Cucumber	074
Courgette	078
Winter Squash	082
Sweetcorn	084

ALLIUMS — 086
Leek	088
Onion	092
Garlic	096
Spring Onion	100

BRASSICAS — 102
Cabbage	104
Chinese Cabbage	107
Cauliflower	110
Broccoli	112
Brussels Sprouts	116
Kale	118
Pak Choi	122
Kohl Rabi	123

LEGUMES — 124
Peas	126
Climbing Beans	130
Dwarf Beans	134
Fava Beans	136

LEAFY GREENS	**138**
Chard	140
Lettuce	142
Spinach	144
Chicory	146
Endive	147
Rocket	148
Mustard	149
HERBS	**150**
How to Grow Annual Herbs	152
How to Grow Perennial Herbs	156
Cooking with Herbs	162
SOFT FRUIT	**170**
Strawberry	172
Raspberry	174
Blackberry	178
Blueberry	182
Gooseberry	186
Blackcurrant	190
Redcurrant	194
Rhubarb	196

EDIBLE FLOWERS	**198**
Why Grow Flowers Too?	200
Nasturtium	202
Rose	204
More Flowers	206
Kitchen Crop Masterplan	208
Resources	216
Index	217
Acknowledgments	222
About the Authors	223

Introduction

What is a good cookbook without tips on sourcing the best ingredients? What is a gardening book without recipes for how to make the most of your harvests? For us, these are two sides of the same coin, and the only way to enjoy real food.

How to grow and cook with the very best food money can't buy – this is your homegrower's companion, taking you crop by crop through about 70 vegetables, fruits, herbs, and flowers.

We wanted to create a handy resource packed with growing and cooking information. Each crop guide tells you how many plants you can grow in a square metre and the estimated harvests so it is flexible to suit your space, no matter how small or big.

Each crop guide also includes recommended varieties for best growing (they're reliable and easy to source) and for best flavour. Storing and preserving techniques mean you can enjoy your harvests through the year and in ways you've likely never heard of before.

Throughout this book, there are three defining principles that have led each and every decision we've made.

1. Nourishment Provide the most nutritious food and best quality of life for us and our environment.

2. Refinement Focus on what works and the practical skills that support it, cutting out the fuss.

3. Presence Promote awareness and fulfilment that leads to a peaceful and joyous life.

With half the book dedicated to the garden and half dedicated to the kitchen, there is little more motivation we can offer than the promise of great food, the joy of growing, cooking, and eating it, and the quality of life that comes with it.

How to
Grow Food

Growing Essentials

Having the right tools and equipment makes gardening more enjoyable and efficient. Here we share the essentials needed to grow everything covered in this book.

SEEDS

The quality of your seeds has a direct impact on the quality of the plants you grow. In resources (see p.216) we list our recommended seed suppliers. If possible, source seeds from local producers as their seeds will be more suited to your climate.

POTS AND TRAYS

There are four core types of pots and module cells we use to sow all of the crops we grow from seed that are mentioned in this book.

To keep it simple, the module cells used in this book are all 4cm (1½in) diameter. Some deep-rooted plants, such as runner beans, require deep module cells, which are specified.

When transplanting seedlings to grow on before planting out, we use 7cm (3in) and 9cm (3½in) pots. For larger containers in which to grow crops to maturity, see page 13.

HEAT AND LIGHT

Seeds that need starting early in the growing season, such as chillies and some other fruiting vegetables, will benefit from a heated propagator and artificial lights. A heated propagator can sit on an indoor windowsill and provide base heat to germinate seeds and encourage growth. Artificial grow lights then prevent seedlings from growing leggy (when they grow too tall and thin in an effort to reach light). There are many different options for heat and light, so find a setup that suits your space and budget (see also resources, p.216).

COMPOST

We start all of our seeds in peat-free multipurpose compost. There are differing qualities of compost out there so speak to gardeners in your area to see what they use and recommend. We list our recommendations for the UK in the resources (see p.216). For any potting on we use the same compost as for seeds, or our homemade compost; see pp.14–15 for more on making compost.

LABELS

It is so important to label what you grow clearly so you know what everything is, particularly so that you can make a note of varieties you want to grow again.

Tip
For writing on labels, we recommend the Staedtler Lumocolor Fine Permanent Pen, which doesn't fade in the sun.

MINI-GREENHOUSE

A mini-greenhouse is a shelving unit with a clear plastic cover and a large access flap. It's useful for storing sown module trays, and housing seedlings as they grow. Outside, it's best placed against a south-facing wall, and opened for ventilation on sunny spring days and all day from early summer, but always closed at night. In a polytunnel, having the cover will give you double insulation, allowing seeds to be sown even earlier; the cover can be removed from mid-spring once temperatures rise.

POLYTUNNEL

A polytunnel extends the growing season and allows you to have more success with warmth-loving plants such as tomatoes. You can also grow salads through winter in a polytunnel. Even a small polytunnel will make a big difference, and low-cost polytunnels work provided that you anchor them thoroughly to the ground with weights and pins.

TOOLS

You only need a few tools for a successful garden! Here are our top 10 essential tools:

1. Trowel*
2. Spade
3. Fork
4. Rake
5. Watering can*
6. Secateurs*
7. Shears
8. Harvesting knife*
9. Wheelbarrow
10. Hose setup

Optional extras
1. Herb snips*
2. Shovel

* also for container growing

Tip
If you have the opportunity, borrow a few tools from a friend so you can see which styles to get – for example, do you prefer a shorter-handled spade over a long-handled one?

Techniques for Growing

Here, we cover how to successfully grow your own food and ways to support crops at different stages of growth for the best yield. Not all plants require all techniques, but these are the primary ones you will come across in this book.

SOWING

Seeds are sown either directly into the ground, usually in a trench, or in modules filled with peat-free multipurpose compost (usually under cover) to then pot on (see right) or transplant (see opposite). Different seeds need different depths, which are given in the growing information for each crop in the book.

After sowing, it is vital to not let the compost dry out before seedlings appear as this can greatly reduce their success rate. If sowing directly, you may need to thin out excess seedlings (gently pulling them out or cutting them at the base) to the ideal spacing to give the remaining seedlings room to mature.

POTTING ON

Potting on is where you move a seedling on from a module or smaller pot into a bigger pot to give it more space and time to grow before being planted out (pictured left). More time could be needed to wait for temperatures to warm up, to give the seedling more resilience against slugs, or to wait for space in the garden. There are two signs that seedlings need potting on: the roots are coming out of the drainage holes; and, when you gently take the seedling out of its pot, roots are starting to spiral around the edge of the compost.

WATERING

Aim to water as early in the morning as possible (if not, late afternoon into evening). Water close to the base of the plant for most efficiency. If you are planting larger plants like peppers and tomatoes, use your hands to create a bowl shape in the soil around the stem of the plant so that when you water the bowl captures the water and allows it to move down into the soil rather than run off and away from the roots.

Plants have different watering needs according to their growing stages:

Sown seeds Keep the soil or compost moist but not soaked.

Seedlings Water module and in-ground seedlings when the top 1cm (½in) of soil or compost is dry to touch.

Maturing plants Water in the first 4–6 weeks after transplanting when the top 2–3cm (1in) of soil is dry. Do the same for direct-sown maturing plants after 3–4 weeks from germination.

Mature plants Once plants have established well they generally need to be watered only when the top 5cm (2in) of soil is dry.

HARDENING OFF

Around a week before planting out any seedlings, bring them outside during the day and then return them under cover for the night. For the first two or three days place them out in a semi-shady spot, and then for another two or three days place them in the open before planting them out in their final position. This process reduces transplant shock, and also toughens up plants against slug damage.

TRANSPLANTING

Transplanting can be done any time of day provided you give the plants plenty of water as soon as they are in the ground, or in containers to mature. Hungry plants such as squash will benefit from a couple of handfuls of compost placed at the base of the planting hole.

FROST PROTECTION

Many of the plants in this book, such as courgettes, will be killed if they get frosted. These are labelled as half hardy or tender in the key growing information; half hardy plants will only survive a light frost. Use the map listed in the resources (see p.216) to find out your last and first average frost dates, and avoid planting out tender crops until a couple of weeks after your last average frost date. Keep an eye on temperature and use eco-horticultural fleece to cover plants on nights when frost threatens.

MULCHING

Mulching retains moisture, reduces weeds, and offers a slow release of nutrients. It's recommended for perennial plants (those that live for 3 years or more, like blackcurrants and rosemary). We are also big advocates of mulching as many of your vegetables as possible. Single-stemmed vegetables like kale and leeks are easiest to mulch, but you can also mulch between rows of seedlings and around clumps of plants.

Whenever you mulch around a plant, aim for a layer of 5cm (2in) minimum, and leave a 5cm (2in) gap around the stem to allow it to breathe and avoid potential disease issues. The best mulch materials are leaves, grass clippings, straw, woodchip (see resources, p.216), and well-rotted manure. You can also mulch with compost; for more on fertility needs, see page 12.

Key growing information

The following symbols are used with the key growing information for each crop.

- 🌱 Sowing time
- ⚓ Planting time
- ↕ Sowing depth
- ↔ Space between plants
- 📅 Time from sowing to first harvest
- ☼ Light needs
- ❄ Temperature needs
- 💧 Water needs
- 🌿 Fertility needs
- ▢ Plants per sq m
- 🧺 Yield per sq m

Growing in Beds & Containers

There are many options when it comes to the types of garden beds and containers in which you can grow food. If you have the space, growing in beds is best, but you can still grow food on a patio or balcony, thanks to containers.

RAISED BEDS
These sided beds are raised off the ground, usually around 30cm (1ft). You can buy or make taller ones – though these take far more material to fill. Raised beds require less bending over than beds in the ground, don't have encroaching grass problems, and help keep crops organized.

An ideal size to aim for is 3 x 1.2m (10 x 4ft) as this is narrow enough to reach the centre from both sides, yet not so narrow that you are tempted to "hop" over and risk damaging plants.

IN-GROUND BEDS
Made by either removing turf and then mixing compost into the topsoil, or adding layers of cardboard over a lawn and then a 10cm (4in) thick layer of compost, in-ground beds tend to cost less to create due to having no physical sides. Provided you keep on top of encroaching grass with an edger, in-ground beds give you more freedom than sided beds to make them the size and shape you want.

FERTILITY NEEDS
We've categorized fertility needs into three – low, medium, and high:

Low No need to add compost if a "high need" crop was grown the previous year; otherwise add around 1–2cm (½in) of compost in late winter to early spring. No feed required.

Medium Add a 2–3cm (1in) layer of compost in late winter to early spring. Feed monthly from mid-spring to early autumn.

High Add a 5cm (2in) layer of compost in late winter to early spring. Feed twice a month during the growing season. Adding two handfuls of compost at the base of the planting hole also helps.

Crops with higher needs require more compost and feed (see box for making your own). If you are looking to purchase liquid feed, then I recommend seaweed feed as a good all-rounder (see resources, p.216).

It's a good idea to keep note of what you grow where

CONTAINERS

For the crop-specific growing advice in this book we usually highlight how many plants to grow in a standard container, and will mention if we recommend a larger one. The standard container size we reference is a 35-litre (7½ gallon) potato container, with a diameter of 43cm (17in). This means you can fit four containers per square metre of patio or balcony space.

When you first grow in containers, fill them with an approximate ratio of 1:1 of topsoil and compost. Before the start of the next growing season, the containers may need to be refreshed for fertility. For low-fertility crops, simply add a 2–3cm (1in) layer of compost to the top of the pot and lightly mix it to a depth of around 10cm (4in). For medium- and high-fertility crops, remove one-third to half of the contents (use this as a brown material in your compost, see p.14) then mix the remaining contents with fresh compost.

Due to the limited soil volume, some more hungry plants in containers will greatly benefit from liquid feeds. Aim to feed all your containers at least monthly in the growing season, and twice a week for hungry crops from early summer.

each year to help you plan out what to grow next year, and what needs the most compost (see the guidelines for each category opposite). It is easier for feeding to grow all the hungry crops together, or at least in blocks. Please note that these are guidelines to maximize production, not rules. If you don't feed your plants, they will still be totally fine, provided they have a decent amount of compost.

Making your own liquid feed

Fill a round dustbin (or similar) with as many of the following plants as possible (a lot are common weeds): nettles, thistles, dandelions, grass, comfrey, and dock. Chop them up roughly before adding them. Then pour in enough water to just cover the plant material. Keep a loose lid over the top. After a month you can begin to use the feed, diluted 1 part liquid to 10 parts water. Continue adding plant material and water over the season for continuous production of the liquid feed.

Making Your Own Compost

Compost, which is made up of organic materials that have decomposed into a nutrient-rich medium full of microbes, is what makes growing your own food possible. By adding compost to your beds and pots, you will ensure your plants enjoy the nutrients they need to grow strong. Making your own is a bit like printing money in slow motion! It's very easy – all you need is a square metre of space, and you are good to go. Mulch and fertility needs are covered in more detail on pages 11–12.

MAKING COMPOST

1. Make a compost bin
Either buy a compost bin ready made, around 1 sq m (3 x 3ft), or build a simple construction by tying 4 pallets (or similar) securely together.

2. Fill it
Fill it with a selection of the green and brown materials listed opposite. Mix these together as you add them, rather than placing them in layers.

3. Wait while the compost matures
Once the compost bin is full of material, you wait. You can speed up the process by turning the material into an adjacent compost bin to help mix everything together. The compost will be ready in 6–12 months.

4. Start a second compost bin (optional)
If you have the space, create a second compost bin to start filling with material while you wait for the first to mature. You can plant a pumpkin in the full compost bin to maximize yield so it doesn't feel like you're sacrificing growing space!

5. Apply the compost
When the compost has become a brown, crumbly texture and smells like a forest floor, it is ready to be used in the garden for sowing, potting up, transplanting, and mulching (see pp.10–11).

ENSURING SUCCESS

There is no such thing as too much homemade compost and, with rising prices of bagged compost, making your own has so many benefits. Here are a couple of ways to make more compost more quickly.

Keep it small

The smaller the material, the faster it will decompose. For example, shredding autumn leaves with a lawnmower, or smashing up kale stems, will help them break down much faster, and create a more consistent compost.

Sourcing materials

Look for opportunities to source materials from your local community, such as veg scraps from a restaurant, or coffee grounds from a café. One person's waste is another person's treasure!

Tip

For small gardens, locate your compost bin(s) in the shadiest corner. Shade is the least valuable growing space. In larger gardens, locate the bin at the top of a slope to make moving heavy compost easier.

Composting ingredients

Aim for a 2:1 ratio of greens to browns, although a 1:1 or 1:2 ratio will also work.

Green materials

Used coffee grounds and plastic-free tea bags

Weeds without seedheads

Grass clippings (unsprayed)

Fruit and vegetable scraps

Horse, cow, rabbit, and chicken manure

Freshly cut plant material

Loose seaweed

Brown materials

Cardboard and newspaper (non-glossy)

Dead and dry plant material

Dust from vacuuming and dryer lint

Sawdust (use sparingly)

Autumn leaves (shredded if possible)

Straw and hay

Spent compost/soil from containers

The Self-Sufficiency Formula

This method lets you calculate exactly how much of any crop to grow, based on your own eating habits, storage capacity, and yield per square metre. This is ideal for staple crops such as roots, alliums, legumes, squash, and cabbages. This is the formula we use, and we have added an example of potatoes to show you how simple it is.

YOUR PRIORITIES

Most gardens aren't big enough to be self-sufficient in every vegetable. However, through our own small space self-sufficiency experiment, we have tested and proven that you can grow about 5 portions of veg a day for 4 people, 365 days a year, in 125sq m (1,350sq ft).

If your vegetable space is smaller, it all comes down to choosing what you wish to be self-sufficient in. Potatoes are relatively cheap to buy, but are usually one of the main staples throughout the year. There is no right or wrong when it comes to choosing what you wish to grow, we just recommend growing things that you enjoy and/or that excite you the most!

1. Work out your weekly need

Next time you eat a vegetable, weigh the portion size in grams to work out what your needs are. If there are different portion sizes in the same household, add the portion sizes together and divide by the number of people to get an average weight.

Formula Average portion size (g) × number of people × portions per week ÷ 1,000 = kg per week

Example 200g × 2 people × 5 portions per week ÷ 1,000 = 2kg per week

2. Work out your annual need

Taking the above figure, work out how many weeks you will realistically be able to eat this crop, taking into account seasonal, fresh produce and preserves.

Formula kg per week × number of weeks you'll eat the crop = total kg needed

Example 2kg × 44 weeks = 88kg per year

The Self-Sufficiency Formula

5. Convert growing space into plant numbers
The final step helps you work out how many seeds to buy or seedlings to raise in order to ensure you have enough plants to fill the growing space.

Formula Growing area × plants per sq m = total plants

Example 15.1sq m × 5 plants/sq m = 76 plants

Feel free to take this formula and adjust it however you see fit. We really hope that this reduces any overwhelm you might have in working out how much of each crop you need.

Do it yourself …

Gather these data points so you can apply this formula to any crop:

Portion size (g)

People

Total portions per week

Weeks per year eating this crop

Yield in kg per sq m (from this book)

Plants per sq m (from this book)

---

3. Add a buffer
Before moving onwards it is important to build in a bit of an insurance policy to take account of potential crop challenges such as weather, pests, and diseases.

Formula Annual kg × 1.2 = adjusted annual kg

Example 88kg × 1.2 = 105.6kg adjusted annual need

4. Convert adjusted annual need into growing space
Use the average yield per square metre provided for each crop in this book to work out the total growing space you need to achieve this weight target.

Formula Adjusted annual kg ÷ yield per sq m = growing area (sq m)

Example 105.6kg ÷ 7kg/sq m = 15.1sq m

How to Grow Food

Polyculture

Polyculture is the opposite of monoculture. Polyculture gardening is where you grow more than one crop in the same space – for example, growing dwarf beans under sweetcorn, or planting a nasturtium in the corner of a raised bed – whereas a field full of one crop (such as wheat or swedes) is a monoculture. A polyculture can be as simple or as complex as you like – but why grow this way?

NATURE-INSPIRED DESIGN

We follow a gardening method known as permaculture, which in a nutshell means nature-inspired design. By observing patterns and systems in nature, we can apply what works in the natural world to help our gardens flourish. When you visit a natural woodland, you observe many types of plants growing together, in many layers. We can draw from this to add an extra dimension to our gardens.

Nature benefits from this diversity in many ways. Firstly it is harder for a pest or disease to cause issues as its host plants aren't all confined to one spot. It also encourages a diversity of insects, which help keep a natural balance of predators and pests. Also, growing in different layers of plant height creates microclimates that other plants can enjoy; for example, shade-loving plants grow under the shade of trees, so why not grow salad in the shade of climbing beans?

POLYCULTURE IN YOUR GARDEN

Polyculture can be as complex as you like, but this can make it much harder to plan and manage as a gardener, and yields will be lower. A balanced approach where you "season" your garden with a little polyculture throughout is the way to go in terms of high yields for self-sufficiency while enjoying the natural benefits in terms of reduced pest and disease issues. And you get one more bonus from this – it fills your garden with colour! Here are five simple polyculture techniques you can use in your garden:

1. Split it up
Where possible, avoid growing a staple crop like potatoes or onions in one single block. Instead, split the potato patch in half and grow each half on different

Polyculture

sides of the garden. This spreads the risk of losing your whole crop to a pest or disease – in other words, you're not putting all your eggs in one basket!

2. Ends and islands
Where crops are taking up a part of a bed, grow annual herbs – whose flowers are adored by insects – and edible flowers among the different vegetables you are growing. You could grow a row of herbs or flowers at the end of a raised bed, or between different crops. You could also plant a clump of annual herbs in the middle of a crop to create a mini biodiversity island.

3. Combinations
Instead of having a square metre each of carrots and onions, grow rows of carrots alternating with onions, for example (pictured below). This takes up no extra space, and is a micro-version of the split-it-up technique. To make your own combinations, grow a taller crop with a shorter one beneath, such as kale with lettuce, so the two crops are not competing.

4. Layers
Think about how you can add interesting layers to your growing space. For example, instead of growing all your climbing beans in one bed, create a few bean structures spread throughout your garden to add variation in height.

5. Plugging gaps
A simple yet effective way of adding polyculture to your garden is to plug gaps that emerge after harvesting with edible flowers and annual herbs (coriander pictured above). It's also a good way to cover up an area of poor germination, or perhaps where an isolated plant has died. The corners of beds are often useful gaps that can be plugged, too.

CONTAINER POLYCULTURE
Even if you can only grow in containers, you can still apply the techniques of polyculture. See the container growing section on page 119 to see how we suggest adding a couple of edible flowers alongside kale to make full use of space. Of course these could be annual herbs, too. Alternatively, for every five containers growing veg, consider one container dedicated to edible flowers and herbs. To avoid blocks, mix up the positioning of containers, so the same crop is not all growing together.

Kitchen Staples

Much as we'd like to, we can't grow everything. Here are some of our favourite kitchen cupboard staples that help us to make the most of homegrown produce.

FOUNDATIONAL
Vinegar Apple cider, malt, white, red, sherry, balsamic, and rice vinegar: these are essential for pickling and provide lively acidity to brighten dishes.

Oil From neutral cooking oils to flavoursome dressing oils, it's a good idea to keep one of each type. Oils are also great for finishing dishes, particularly flavoured ones like herb oil and chilli crisp.

Sea salt This is a kitchen essential for preserving, fermenting, seasoning, and finishing. There are many types of salt, but the only rule is to avoid table salt, which is often filled with anticaking agents, making it unsuitable for preserving and fermenting. Flaky sea salt is a great all-rounder.

Whole peppercorns The world of peppercorns is vast: black, pink, green, white, and many more. Mix them in a mill and add a few twists into most dishes for an aromatic boost.

Citrus Lemon, orange, lime, and more are great ways to lift a meal with acidic zest or juice right before serving.

Soy sauce, tamari, Worcestershire sauce In case you don't have stock, adding a splash of these sauces is a great way to give a bit of depth and umami to a meal.

Miso Another umami bomb, this paste is packed with digestive enzymes and flavour. Add a teaspoonful to sauces and broths to finish.

PRESERVED PROTEINS

Tinned, jarred, or dried beans and lentils One of the simplest ways to add tasty, available protein to a meal is to crack open some beans. It's useful to have extra for when you don't have any in the garden.

Tinned oily fish Sardines, anchovies, and mackerel can all add protein and umami to most vegetable dishes.

Nutritional yeast This is a plant-based ingredient where adding just a teaspoon or two introduces a nutty, cheesy flavour and aroma to dishes.

Dried mushrooms These are a great way to store nutrition and protein, and rehydrating them produces a secondary product – a delicious mushroom stock.

Hard cheese Grated directly into or on top of meals, aged cheeses add creaminess, seasoning, and a whole lot of umami. Save rinds in the freezer and cook them into sauces.

BULK AND CARBS

Pasta Slow-dried and delicious, pasta is one of the simplest ways to bulk out a meal.

Rice Fried, boiled, steamed, or baked, rice is a highly versatile accompaniment to any meal, and is great at absorbing flavours when cooked in the same pot as other ingredients.

Polenta A fine cornmeal, polenta thickens soups, crisps doughs, and bulks out just about anything it touches.

Pearl barley, farro, bulgur This collection of delicious, springy, natural grains can be thrown into soups, broths, and salads by the handful.

Flour For all your pastry and baking needs, flour is vital. Plain and wholemeal are ideal for most dishes, plus strong bread flour for homemade breads.

Kitchen Techniques

The kitchen is the beating heart of a home, a place of craft, artistry, sustenance, and satiation. A good home cook is versatile, sympathetic to the nature of their ingredients and the needs of their household, and, above all, a lifelong learner. Every meal offers a chance to refine a skill: to simmer more gently, roast more evenly, season more intuitively.

With homegrown produce, we are dealing with the most delicious, healthy ingredients. From harvest to plate, there is a single guiding principle underlying each and every technique and recipe in this book: do enough, no more, no less. Elegant pairings and simple techniques are all that is required to unlock the beauty of what nature has already provided.

You won't find exotic produce or lengthy ingredients lists here. Without fuss or show, the recipes in this book are designed to make good, honest food, and bring the beauty of your garden to your dinner plate. Most of us don't have all the time and money in the world to dedicate to meals, but that doesn't mean we must settle for the ordinary.

Before we jump into the recipes in this book, we need to cover some foundational skills. The techniques that follow will show you how to draw out every last drop of flavour from fruit, vegetables, herbs, and flowers – roasting, simmering, fermenting, drying, and preserving them in ways that celebrate their true character, before any remaining scraps make their way to the compost bin.

TIPS DOWN

There is one thing that will dramatically speed up your time spent in the kitchen, and it isn't some newfangled invention or money-hungry gadget. Knife skills. Being proficient with a kitchen knife makes work quick, efficient, and safe. It also means you can start cooking prior to preparing all your ingredients, then keep chopping as you go, which is by far the most time-efficient way to work.

It might feel unnatural at first, but keep the tip of your blade against the chopping board as you work, pivoting around this point as you move the handle up and

Kitchen Techniques

down. This anchors the knife in place, making it safer for you to move quickly without risk of injury.

Holding your ingredients in your non-dominant hand, keep them beneath your palm, and hook your fingers over them. With your fingertips pointing down, forming an arch over the ingredients in a similar shape to a pianist's hand, line up the broad side of the blade against the back of your fingers (pictured above). Now, both hands work together to control each motion. Your dominant hand moves the blade up and down, while your other hand moves backwards, making its way along the ingredient as you go, revealing the amount of ingredient you wish to chop. The blade should always remain in contact with both the board and your hand, and as long as your fingers remain hooked, nothing except your ingredients should be cut.

TECHNIQUES FOR COOKING VEGETABLES

Water-based
Generally, water-based techniques require a lower temperature than other methods, and are used to gently cook ingredients all the way through. Advantages to these methods are that they preserve moisture well while applying an even heat, they're healthy, they allow for greater control with less input, and they offer an opportunity to infuse with additional flavours. The downside is that water will flood your ingredients, diluting flavours and nutrients – but this can work to our advantage. By increasing the mineral content through salting water, or cooking in stocks and broths with additional herbs or spices, we can force an infusion that's a two way exchange, increasing the tastiness of our vegetables.

Boiling Cooking vegetables in rapidly boiling salted water until tender.

Blanching Briefly boiling vegetables, then shocking them in ice water to retain their colour and texture.

Simmering Cooking vegetables gently in water or broth at a lower temperature than boiling (pictured below left).

Steaming Cooking vegetables over, but not in, boiling water, covered with a lid, to preserve nutrients and flavour.

Poaching Gently cooking vegetables in barely simmering water or broth.

Braising Slowly cooking vegetables in a small amount of liquid, often after browning them first through searing or frying.

Stewing Cooking vegetables in a liquid for longer, often with other ingredients (pictured below centre).

Slow-cooking Cooking a whole meal in stock or water at a low temperature for an entire day (often while you are away from the kitchen).

Dry heat
These techniques are all about concentration of flavour and contrasting textures. Through maillard browning (reactions between amino acids and sugars caused by high-heat cooking) and caramelization (pictured below right), ingredients develop deeply savoury qualities that are more intense than water-based techniques. They also form crisp exteriors and tender interiors, losing moisture via evaporation which intensifies flavours compared to the opposite process of dilution in boiling, blanching, and poaching. These techniques also unlock more aromatic compounds in ingredients, often with the introduction of a small amount of fat, boosting our sensory experience where it counts.

Roasting Cooking vegetables in the oven at a high heat to develop caramelization – between 190°C (170°C fan/375°F/Gas 5) and 210°C (190°C fan/410°F/Gas 7).

Baking Similar to roasting, but usually at a lower temperature, sometimes wrapped (for example, baked potatoes).

Kitchen Techniques

Grilling Cooking vegetables under a high-heat source, such as a grill or broiler (pictured above right).

Searing Cooking food at a high heat to brown but not burn its surface through the maillard reaction, creating a savoury, caramelized crust (pictured above left).

Barbecuing Cooking over an open flame or on a grill for a smoky flavour (pictured above centre).

Sautéing Cooking vegetables in a small amount of fat over a medium heat until soft but not browned.

Pan-frying Cooking vegetables in more oil than sautéing, often until crisp.

Stir-frying Cooking quickly over a high heat in a wok with little oil.

Deep-frying Submerging vegetables in hot oil for a crispy exterior (e.g. tempura).

Air-frying Using hot air circulation to cook vegetables with minimal oil.

SPECIALIZED AND PRESERVING

These techniques each go a little further in their own ways. Some use special methods, others particular equipment, but each is useful to know when it comes to bringing versatility to cooking with your own produce.

Sweating Gently cooking vegetables in a covered pan with a little oil or butter to draw out moisture.

Caramelizing Cooking vegetables slowly in a little fat until their natural sugars develop a deep, sweet flavour.

Confit Slowly cooking vegetables submerged in oil or butter at a low temperature.

Smoking Cooking vegetables on a rack over smouldering wood or coals for a deep, smoky flavour. This can be done hot (65–90°C/150–195°F), or cold (below 30°C/86°F), and with different types of wood or herbs for more flavour.

Recipe symbols

The following symbols are used with the recipes under each crop.

▢ Recipe served cold, or for preserving

✎ Recipe for cooking

Charring Exposing vegetables to intense heat (for example, open flame, grill, or dry pan) for a smoky, slightly burnt flavour.

Salt-baking Encasing vegetables in a crust of 1kg (2¼lb) of salt to 3 egg whites, mixed well, then baking them to retain moisture. For a plant-based version, make a salt dough with salt, flour, and water.

Sous vide Vacuum-sealing ingredients, often with butter, seasoning, and herbs, and cooking them gently in a precise temperature-controlled water bath to retain their flavours.

Microwaving Quickly cooking vegetables using electromagnetic radiation, often with a bit of water.

Fermenting Not cooking in the traditional sense, but using beneficial bacteria to develop flavour and preserve (for example, sauerkraut, kimchi).

Pickling Preserving vegetables in vinegar or brine, sometimes with light cooking if the brine is heated before pouring over the ingredients (pictured above).

Dehydrating Removing moisture from vegetables at a low heat for longer preservation (for example, sun-dried tomatoes).

Setting jams Place a spoonful of hot, freshly made jam or jelly on a chilled plate, let it cool briefly, then push it with your finger. If it wrinkles, it's ready.

Sterilizing jars Washing jars thoroughly in hot, soapy water, rinsing well, then placing them in an oven at 140°C (275°F) for 20–30 minutes until completely dry.

SAUCES

Sauces can be defined as anything runnier than the ingredients they're paired with, and involve a host of techniques. Sauces often make a meal, and their absence often breaks one. A flavourless broth, a dry roast, or a bland salad are each fixed with the addition of sauces. They're a great waste saver, too, as you can blend scraps into a sauce or dip. Pan sauces are a joy: when you've finished cooking in a pan, tip a little water or wine into the hot pan and scrape up all those tasty bits that were stuck around the edges before pouring it over your plated dish. And there's no need to be a snob. Not all sauces need to be homemade. If your soup is lacking a little life, why not reach for a bottle of hot sauce?

There are, of course, plenty of homemade sauce recipes later in the book, turning the very best of your garden harvests into dinner-saving powerhouses of flavour.

MASTER STOCK METHOD

A good stock is so much more than a means to reduce waste in the kitchen. It is the backbone to many other dishes, providing depth and body. It's also the perfect way to use up all those veg scraps you've been saving in the freezer.

Makes 3–4 litres (5–7 pints)

Ingredients

2kg (4$\frac{1}{2}$lb) bones (beef, chicken carcasses, or fish frames) or 1.5kg (3lb 3oz) mixed vegetables (onions, carrots, celery)

2 onions (halved, skins on), 2 carrots, 2 celery sticks, roughly chopped

250ml (9fl oz) wine (red for beef, white for chicken/fish)

2 or 3 bay leaves, 6–8 black peppercorns, a few thyme sprigs

1 bulb of garlic, halved widthways

2–3 tbsp tomato purée (for beef or chicken)

1. Scale the fish bones to remove bitter slime (to do this, rinse the bones, remove any skin, gills, and fins, and clean well). Scald chicken or beef bones to reduce scum later on (to scald the bones, briefly cover the bones with cold water, bring to the boil, then drain and rinse). Roast beef or chicken bones at 200°C (180°C fan/400°F/Gas 6) for 40 minutes. For fish and vegetable stocks, skip the roasting stage.

2. Put bones (if using) and vegetables in a large pot, add wine, and boil hard for 5 minutes to burn off the rawness, then cover with cold water.

3. Bring to a bare simmer (never a rolling boil) and skim off the scum that rises to the surface.

4. Then add herbs, peppercorns, garlic, and tomato purée and simmer gently: beef for 6–12 hours, chicken for 3–4 hours, fish for 30–40 minutes, and vegetable stock for 45–60 minutes.

5. Strain through a fine sieve, chill, and skim the fat. Reduce further if desired for a richer demi-glace sauce.

Tip
You can swap the wine for cider, sherry, or beer (when they have finished cooking, no alcohol is left). Add dried mushrooms, kombu, or yeast extract for umami (especially in vegetable stock).

Meal prep
Freeze stock in ice cube trays for quick use.

Root Vegetables

Root Vegetables

Potato

Key growing information

- Early spring to midsummer
- 15cm (6in) sowing depth
- 35cm (14in) between first earlies; 40cm (16in) between second earlies; 45cm (18in) between maincrop
- 12–16 weeks to harvest
- Full sun
- Tender
- Medium water needs
- High fertility needs
- 5–7 plants per sq m
- 6–12kg (13–26½lb) per sq m

Recommended varieties

First early (new potatoes, ready in 12 weeks) 'Accent' (well-textured, waxy), 'Swift' (dependable, named for its growth rate, waxy); **Second early** (ready in 13–15 weeks) 'Charlotte' (pictured far right, salad potato, easy to grow, high yields, clean harvests, waxy), 'Vivaldi' (fantastic for taste and texture, balanced between waxy and floury); **Maincrop** (ready after 16 weeks) 'King Edward' (reliable for roasting, floury), 'Sarpo Mira' (productive, blight-resistant, floury), 'Sarpo Java' (productive, blight-resistant, between waxy and floury)

Growing

While there are so many different ways of growing potatoes, the techniques we share here will work for any variety. To encourage first early crops, you can "chit" potatoes by putting them somewhere light indoors in midwinter to encourage them to sprout before planting under cover either in beds or containers. This is needed only for a very early crop otherwise, just plant them and they will grow!

Tip
If you are after high yields and winter abundance, opt for maincrop potatoes. A few will grow large enough to be jacket potatoes.

STAGE 1

Dig a hole about 20cm (8in) deep and wide, and add a 5cm (2in) layer of compost or well-rotted manure at the base. Give the hole a generous watering and **place a seed potato** on the compost before filling the hole back in. When planting, space maincrops further apart than first earlies as they will need more room to develop.

STAGE 2

Once leaves appear, **protect** early plantings from frost. If it is forecast, cover the leaves with a thick layer of grass clippings or straw, and remove the following day.

STAGE 3
Mulch plants once the canopy has closed (when you can't see soil between plants), with a generous mulch of 5cm (2in) depth of grass clippings or similar to retain soil moisture. This mulch will also decompose and add fertility to the soil.

CONTAINER GROWING
Plant 2 first earlies or 1 maincrop potato in each container. Mulch after planting with a 5cm (2in) layer of grass clippings to retain moisture (pictured above left). **Water** every other day in dry weather. To **harvest**, simply empty the container into a wheelbarrow and pick out the potatoes (pictured above).

HARVEST
When the plants begin to flower, start to harvest the potatoes, though for the best maincrop yields, harvest once the plants begin to turn yellow in early autumn. Use a fork to gently lift the plant as you use your other hand to pull it out of the soil. Thoroughly rummage through the soil so you don't leave any potatoes behind.

To dry potatoes, place them for a few hours in sunlight (turning them over at least once) and then place them into breathable hessian sacks. Do not wash the spuds as the soil will help them store for longer and do not store any damaged potatoes. Keep the sacks in a cool, dry, and dark place to store for up to 7 months.

Root Vegetables

Look out for
Dark lesions on the stems and leaves of potato plants are a sign of potato blight. Remove the affected leaves immediately, and once over a third of the plant is impacted it is best to harvest and store your crop so the blight doesn't get to the potatoes themselves.

Blighted leaves can be placed on the compost. New potatoes rarely get impacted due to their earlier harvest in the season, and growing blight-resistant maincrop varieties is the best way to avoid losses.

Potato scab causes blistering on potato skins and occurs when there hasn't been enough moisture. Remedy this by ensuring your plants are well watered. Mulching (stage 3) will also reduce scab issues. If you do get potato scab, peel off affected areas and cook as usual.

Cooking

Potatoes are king in many cuisines, and with good reason. Everyone has a favourite way to cook them, from a clean new potato salad, with mayonnaise and chives, to a humble jacket potato. There are loaded wedges, saag aloo, creamy dauphinoise, kartoffelpuffer, tartiflette (see p.45), and gnocchi – never mind the numerous ways to mash, roast, steam, purée, and fry. Some varieties are better suited to particular uses: generally, new potatoes and salad varieties are waxy, and mature potatoes are floury (see also p.32).

GRILLED POTATO BUNS

Yoghurty, slow proved, soft, and buttery, these buns can be made ahead of time. They store in a fridge for up to 2 days before baking, or you can freeze them once baked to enjoy at a later date.

Makes 24

Ingredients

825g (1¾lb) floury potatoes

30g (1oz) sea salt

450g (1lb) natural yoghurt

50g (1¾oz) fresh yeast

825g (1¾lb) plain flour

80g (3oz) melted butter

1. Roughly chop each potato into 8 pieces. If you want a smooth bun, remove the skins, but I prefer the rustic look. Simmer them in boiling water for 20 minutes until soft, then drain.

2. Tip them back into the pan they cooked in and mash them with salt, then allow to cool for 10 minutes.

3. Add the mash to a bowl, with the yoghurt, yeast, and flour (pictured below top left), and knead (below top right) until the dough forms a smooth ball (bottom).

4. Cover and leave at room temperature (at or above 18°C/64°F) for 2–3 hours, then knock it back, reshape,

and store in a fridge until needed (for up to 2 days).

5. Remove the dough from the fridge 2 hours before you plan to shape it, then cut into 24 equal pieces, each weighing about 80–85g (3oz).

6. Pull the edges of each piece into the middle, and roll it beneath your palm, seam-side down, into a ball. To prevent dough sticking to your hands, dampen them slightly with water or oil.

7. Place each ball on a lined baking tray and let them rest for up to 2 hours. Preheat a grill and the oven to 210°C (190°C fan/410°F/Gas 7).

8. Pop each bun on the grill for 1–2 minutes. Once they have a crust and light char (pictured below bottom left), flip them to repeat on the other side. Remove from the grill, brush with melted butter (pictured below top left), then bake on the lined tray for 10–15 minutes.

Tip
If you're in a rush you can skip grilling the buns (step 8), and bake them right away in the oven.

Meal prep
Once baked, you can freeze them for long-term storage. To use, defrost overnight in a fridge. Rinse with cold water before heating them in an oven at 200°C (180°C fan/400°F/Gas 6) for 5 minutes. Perfect with compound butter (see p.164).

Potato

🔪 TORTILLA

When I was cheffing in a Spanish tapas restaurant, I learned that a good tortilla is cooked very hot, briefly turned, then allowed to rest and finish cooking on the plate. The best are almost a savoury set custard.

Makes 12 portions

Ingredients

Olive oil

900g (2lb) floury potatoes, peeled and chopped into 0.5–1cm (¼–½in) discs

1 onion, diced

Large pinch of sea salt

8–10 eggs, well stirred

1. Heat about 1cm (½in) of oil in a frying pan over a high heat. Pile in the potatoes and onions and add the salt.

2. Keep the pan hot and stir often until the potatoes soften (about 20–30 minutes). Pour in the eggs.

3. While the eggs are still liquid, gently prise apart the potato discs to allow the egg to fill the gaps. After 1 minute, flip the tortilla onto a plate and slide it back into the pan for another minute to seal the other side. Take care and use oven gloves when doing this as hot oil can spill.

4. Once cooked, leave it to stand for 30 minutes before eating. This allows the residual heat from the potato to cook the eggs within.

🔪 LANCASHIRE HOTPOT

Another of my favourite ways to use homegrown potatoes is in the style of a Lancashire hotpot. Take any thick, hearty vegetable stew with lots of sauce and tip it in a casserole dish. Line the top with slices of potato, and brush with melted butter or dripping so that it looks like shining fish scales.

Bake it at 140°C (120°C fan/275°F/Gas 1) for 90 minutes, then remove the lid and let the potatoes crisp up for another 8–10 minutes.

Root Vegetables

Carrot

Key growing information

- Mid-spring to midsummer
- 1cm (½in) sowing depth
- 5cm (2in) between plants
- 10 weeks to harvest
- Full sun
- Hardy
- Medium water needs
- Medium fertility needs
- 100 plants per sq m
- 10kg (22lb) per sq m

Recommended varieties

Early maturing 'Nantes', 'Amsterdam'; **Maincrop** 'Autumn King', 'Flyaway' (carrot root fly resistant), 'Resistafly' (carrot root fly resistant)

Growing

One of the most satisfying experiences in gardening is grabbing a clump of carrot tops, pulling, and revealing a handful of bright orange carrots. Delicious both raw and cooked, and very productive, carrots are much loved for good reason.

STAGE 1

Use the back of a rake to create shallow drills around 1cm (½in) deep, spacing rows 20cm (8in) apart. **Sow** carrot seeds around 2cm (¾in) apart, cover with soil, and gently firm down the soil. **Water** well.

Tip

Carrots need constant moisture for consistent germination. To help with this, gently place a plank over the newly sown row to reduce evaporation. Check daily, and remove the plank as soon as carrot seedlings make an appearance.

STAGE 2

Once the seedlings have developed a couple of true leaves, **thin** them to 1 plant approximately every 5cm (2in) along the row. You can eat the thinnings as a microgreen once rinsed – roots and all!

STAGE 3

As the plants mature, use a hoe to **weed** between rows – this reduces competition. Consider applying a 2–3cm (1in) thick **mulch** of grass clippings to retain moisture.

CONTAINER GROWING

Sow seeds thinly on the surface of a full standard container (spaced around 1–2cm (½in) apart) and cover with an additional 1cm (½in) of compost. Keep well watered. Once a little forest of seedlings has sprung up, **thin** to every 4–5cm (2in). Consider sowing a couple of containers under cover in early spring for an earlier

harvest, bringing out the containers when the weather warms.

HARVEST

Carrots are ready to harvest when their shoulders (the top, from where the leaves emerge) are around 2–3cm (1in) or more in diameter. Pull them out by holding the leaves and pulling upwards. A clever trick to harvest stubborn carrots without using a fork is to push the carrot down by its shoulders before pulling out – the push–pull technique. Try it for yourself and see just how incredibly effective this is! Store lifted carrot roots in sand (see p.47). The leaves are delicious steamed with a little salted butter, or turned into pesto or chopped into salads when raw.

Look out for

Carrot root flies are low-flying pests that adore carrots, and their maggots burrow through the roots. Avoid disasters by choosing resistant varieties (like 'Resistafly' or 'Flyaway'), growing in containers 60cm (2ft) above the ground, or creating a 60cm (2ft) tall barrier of insect mesh around your carrot patch.

Cooking

CARROT MISO HUMMUS

Hummus is a fantastic way to celebrate raw vegetables. You can use it as a dip, a sandwich filling, or even add a spoonful or two into soups, casseroles, and pie fillings for a creamy lemony kick. I add miso to hummus as seasoning, as the saltiness fulfills the role of sea salt, but miso also brings with it additional flavour, umami, and digestive enzymes, making for a fuller, more delicious hummus.

Makes 440g (1lb)

Ingredients
1 tbsp cumin seeds

250g (9oz) cooked chickpeas (see tip)

1 large lemon (60ml/2fl oz juice)

60ml (2fl oz) light tahini

50ml (1¾fl oz) extra virgin olive oil

2 or 3 raw garlic cloves (see tip)

2 tbsp cold water or aquafaba

1 tbsp white miso

1 medium carrot, washed and grated, leaves reserved

1. Lightly toast the cumin seeds for 4–5 minutes in a frying pan until they release their aroma.

2. Tip the cumin and everything else except the carrot and a tablespoon of the olive oil into a food processor and blend until smooth. If the mixture is too thick, add more of the cold water (or aquafaba) to loosen it up. Adjust the seasoning.

3. Blend the grated carrot into the hummus until smooth.

4. To serve, generously spoon the hummus onto a plate and spread it to form valleys. Dress with the additional olive oil, and top with chopped carrot leaves, or serve with grated pickled carrot (see p.51).

Tip
For the best hummus, use dried chickpeas and cook them yourself. This can take a long time, but you can speed it up if you have a pressure cooker. Reserve some of the cooking water (aquafaba).

Tip
If 2 or 3 raw garlic cloves are too much for you, slow roast a whole bulb, which turns it mellow and buttery. To do this, chop the top off and add a little olive oil. Cover and cook at 200°C (180°C fan/400°F/Gas 6) for 50 minutes. Squeeze out the cooked garlic from several cloves into your hummus – the garlic comes out as a soft purée.

Alternative recipe
While this recipe is for a carrot hummus, feel free to get creative and swap the carrot for beetroot, kohl rabi, chilli, fennel, or mustard. You can also swap out the cumin seeds for coriander, or make the most of fresh herbs in the summer with dill, parsley, chives, sage, and oregano.

Meal prep
Once made, the hummus will last in a fridge for 7 days. You can also freeze hummus for 6–8 months but, depending on the vegetables you use, it may need mixing again to incorporate the extra moisture from thawing.

Parsnip

Key growing information

- Mid- to late spring
- 1–2cm (½–¾in) sowing depth
- 15cm (6in) between plants
- 20 weeks to harvest
- Full sun
- Hardy
- Medium water needs
- Medium fertility needs
- 40 plants per sq m
- 10kg (22lb) per sq m

Recommended varieties

'Tender and True' (pictured right), 'Gladiator'

Growing

Parsnips need patience, but provide you with harvests all winter. Frosts sweeten the roots too, turning starches to sugars. Leave a couple of parsnips behind to flower next year; they are much loved by beneficial insects.

STAGE 1
Sow one seed every 2–3cm (1in) along a trench, cover with soil, and **water** well. Space rows 20cm (8in) apart. Parsnip seedlings can take a few weeks to appear. Use the carrot plank tip (see p.38) to avoid sporadic germination, which can be common. **Thin** to the strongest seedling every 7–8cm (3in) once seedlings have 4 or 5 true leaves.

STAGE 2
In late summer, **thin** every second seedling to allow the remaining roots plenty of space. You can eat the roots of the thinnings.

STAGE 3
In late autumn the tops will begin to die down. **Mulch** with grass clippings or leaves to keep down weeds.

CONTAINER GROWING
Make 8 holes, 2–3cm (1in) deep, and about 15cm (6in) apart, drop 2 seeds in each, cover, and keep watered. **Thin** to the strongest and harvest when ready.

HARVEST
After the first frosts, use the push–pull technique (see p.39) or push a fork into the ground 10cm (4in) away from the plant and prise it up. You can leave them in the ground until you are ready to use them or store them in sand (see p.47).

Look out for
Parsnip canker is a fungal pathogen that can rot roots, especially in damp, cool weather. Avoid by growing in well-draining soil, and in different locations each year.

Cooking

🔪 PARSNIP PURÉE

You might wonder, why am I learning to make parsnip purée? Purées are a great option for root vegetables such as parsnips, carrots, or radishes that are a little too mature and have become woody and fibrous. Once made, a purée is easily frozen and stored for 3–4 months, making it an ideal alternative to roasting, steaming, mashing, and other cooking methods.

Makes 600g (1lb 5oz)

Ingredients

50g (1¾oz) unsalted butter

500g (1lb 2oz) parsnips, peeled and chopped into evenly sized chunks

200ml (7fl oz) double cream

Sea salt and freshly ground pepper

1. Melt the butter in a saucepan over a medium–low heat then add the parsnips and cook for 20–25 minutes, covered, until tender. Stir a few times to avoid burning.

2. While the parnips are still warm, add the double cream and stir until combined. Purée the parsnips using a food processor or immersion blender until smooth. For an extra silky finish, pass the purée through a sieve.

3. Season with salt and freshly ground pepper to taste.

4. Allow the purée to cool completely before portioning into airtight containers or freezer bags. Freeze for 3–4 months.

Meals with …

Purées are delicious incorporated into sauces, soups, and pie fillings. Defrost in the fridge overnight before using. Here are some ideas.

Soups and broths Use a large spoonful as a thickener and creamy enrichment.

Bread dough Add to bread doughs, such as the potato bun recipe, swapping it for some of the potato (see p.35).

Pies and tarts Add some purée to fillings such as the winter squash galette (see p.83).

Fish dishes Use purée to form a side or base to fish dishes.

Swede

Key growing information

- Mid-spring to early summer
- 1–2cm (½–¾in) sowing depth
- 20cm (8in) between plants
- 24 weeks to harvest
- Full sun
- Hardy
- Medium water needs
- Medium fertility needs
- 15 plants per sq m
- 7.5–12kg (16½–26½lb) per sq m

Recommended varieties
'Best of All', 'Lomond', 'Tweed'

Growing

STAGE 1
Sowing direct
We get the highest yields from direct sowing. Create seed drills using the handle of a rake. If you are growing in rows, space them 30cm (12in) apart. **Sow** thinly, one every 1–2cm (½–¾in), cover with the displaced soil, and **water** thoroughly. Seedlings should appear within a week. **Thin** once they have their first set of true leaves to one every 10cm (4in), and enjoy thinnings in a salad!

Sowing in modules
Sow 2 seeds per cell and **thin** to the strongest once there are 4 or 5 true leaves.

STAGE 2
Water deeply if it hasn't rained for 4 or 5 days. **Weed** every couple of weeks, and give a liquid **feed** monthly.

STAGE 3
From late summer, once swede leaves create a closed canopy over the soil, don't worry about weeds or watering. **Harvest** every other swede as a mini-crop in late summer, leaving the bigger of the two to reach full size.

CONTAINER GROWING
Grow 2 or 3 large swedes per container. To **sow**, make three 2cm (¾in) deep holes 15–20cm (6–8in) apart, pop in two to three seeds, cover, then **thin** to the strongest.

HARVEST
Twist and pull plants to harvest from late autumn to late winter. You can sauté the leaves as an additional crop. Leave in a couple of plants until spring for a harvest of leaves during the hungry gap, followed by edible flower shoots. Store roots in sand (see p.47).

Look out for
If dry, flea beetle damage may occur (see p.52). Cabbage white butterflies may eat leaves (see p.105).

Cooking

SWEDE TARTIFLETTE

This vegetarian version of a winter warmer is a cheesy tartiflette that works with any root vegetable or cauliflower. For a tangy contrast, add chopped pickled cucumbers or kimchi. Traditionally made with Reblochon cheese, it can also be made with Saval, Comté, or Raclette.

Serves 4–5

Ingredients

1 onion, finely chopped

3 garlic cloves, finely chopped

40g (1¼oz) herb compound butter (see p.164)

2kg (4½lb) swede (or parsnip/potato/squash) peeled and sliced into 8mm (½in) pieces

350g (12oz) cheese, cut into wedges, rind on

150g (5½oz) pickled cucumber or kimchi

250ml (9fl oz) single cream

Freshly ground black pepper

1. Preheat the oven to 200°C (180°C fan/400°F/Gas 6). Fry the onion and garlic in butter over a medium heat in a large ovenproof dish.

2. Add the swede slices to the pan and cook for another 10–15 minutes.

3. Layer the vegetables, half of the cheese, and pickled cucumber or kimchi into the ovenproof dish. Pour over the cream and season with pepper, then top with the remaining cheese.

4. Bake, covered, for 1 hour 20 minutes, then 10 minutes uncovered until crispy. Serve with winter salad and slaw.

Tip
You could also add a handful of chopped kale or spinach at step 2, and add some parsnip purée (see p.43) at step 3.

Meal prep
Make up to step 2 in bulk, then refrigerate or freeze to finish later. Defrost the night before, complete the steps, then bake for 1 hour 30 minutes at 190°C (170°C fan/375°F/Gas 5).

Beetroot

Key growing information

- 🌱 Mid-spring to midsummer
- ↕ 2cm (³/₄in) sowing depth
- ↔ 7–10cm (2³/₄–4in) between plants, 25cm (10in) for clumps
- 📅 12 weeks to harvest
- ☀ Full sun
- ❄ Hardy
- 💧 Medium water needs
- 🌿 Medium fertility needs
- ▢ 50 plants per sq m
- 🧺 6.25kg (14lb) per sq m

Recommended varieties

Classic beetroot 'Boltardy' (pictured right), 'Detroit 2'; **Cylindrical shape** 'Cylindra'; **Colours and patterns** 'Avalanche', 'Choggia'; **Sweetest tasting** 'Boldor', 'Burpees'

Growing

Most people think beetroot is a bit earthy and bitter, yet homegrown beetroot will transform your perspective on how sweet and delicious this vegetable is. You can take this a step further by exploring all the different varieties available.

STAGE 1

Sowing direct
Sow thinly (every 2–3cm/ ³/₄–1¹/₄in) along rows 20cm (8in) apart, cover, and water thoroughly.

Sowing in modules
Multisow 3 seeds per cell, cover, and **water** thoroughly. Each beetroot "seed" can contain several seeds, so **thin** multisown clumps of more than 5 plants.

STAGE 2

When sown direct
Weed regularly as the seedlings mature, and **water** well during dry weather. When the seedlings have 4 or 5 true leaves, **thin** to their final spacing and eat the leaves of the thinnings either in a salad, or thrown into a stir-fry as you would for spinach.

When sown in modules
Once seedlings have a couple of true leaves, they are ready to **plant out** in clumps into their final growing position. Make holes 25cm (10in) apart slightly larger than the size of the rootball, gently pressing the roots of the clump into each hole so it creates a small indentation in the bed, and **water** well.

STAGE 3

As the roots begin to swell, there is no need to weed further as the mature plants will not be impacted. In a prolonged dry spell, **water** as

047

(see p.141). Store beetroot roots in sand (see box).

Look out for
From late autumn, rodents such as voles will sometimes gnaw on the roots as a food source. Keep an eye out, and if you notice any damage, harvest the whole crop and bring it into storage.

How to store root crops in sand

If you have an unheated garage, cellar, or a cool garden shed, you can store certain root crops, including beetroot, in wooden boxes or crates filled with moist (not wet) sand. Add a 5cm (2in) layer of sand at the base of a box, then space the roots out so they aren't touching. Fill around and over each root with sand, and build up layers of roots until you reach the top of the box. Place a few layers of cardboard over the box to reduce evaporation. Uncover each root as you need it. Use this method to store roots for many months; it is perfect for storing staples like carrots for up to 6 months. The sand can be reused every season too! In spring, the roots may begin to naturally sprout but they are still edible.

---

needed early in the morning then mulch with grass clippings or straw. This helps the plant to produce larger roots, reducing evaporation and keeping soil cool.

CONTAINER GROWING
Direct **sow** 1 seed every 5cm (2in), cover with 1cm (1/2in) of compost, and begin to harvest the bigger roots, allowing the smaller ones to develop. Alternatively, **transplant** 4 clumps of module-sown seedlings per container at equal spacing and **water** well; they don't need thinning. Expect 8–10 decent-sized beetroot.

HARVEST
Beetroot is a proper tip-to-root or zero-waste crop: you can harvest its leaves, roots, and stems. Leaves can be harvested within a matter of weeks – just take one young leaf per plant to use as a salad green. Begin to harvest roots at a desired size, taking larger roots first to allow the smaller ones to continue developing. Harvest by gently twisting the plant until it pulls away from the ground. When you harvest the roots, trim off the mature leaves, which can be eaten with the stems in the same way you would for chard

Cooking

Earthy, sweet beetroot can transform more than the colour of your meals (and hands). The different varieties boast a wide range of flavours, colours, and textures, each uniquely delicious cooked or raw. They can be grated into a salad, or thinly sliced using a mandolin, pickled with sherry vinegar and cracked peppercorns, or slowly cooked down into a thick, glossy ketchup. Bake them into a chocolate fudge brownie (one of the winning recipes in our previous book, *The Self-Sufficiency Garden*), or blend them into hummus (see p.40). Beetroot is the first step towards a better meal no matter what you're making.

SLOW-ROASTED BEETROOT SALAD

One of my favourite ways to enjoy beetroot, which also happens to work well in the embers of a campfire, is slow baked. Roasted over a low heat, the ruby-red flesh of these plump roots is soft and intensely sweet, pairing well with the tart, fruity kick of balsamic vinegar.

Serves 4

Ingredients

5 large beetroot, scrubbed to remove soil

2 red onions, roughly chopped

1 blood orange, halved and juiced

½ tsp mixed peppercorns

Pinch of smoked salt

Drizzle of extra virgin olive oil

100g (3½oz) rocket

Balsamic vinegar

A few dill or fennel fronds

1. Preheat the oven to 140°C (120°C fan/275°F/Gas 1). Remove the beetroot tops (reserve for later).

2. Place the whole beetroot onto a baking tray.

3. Add the onion and orange halves (but not the juice) to the tray with the beetroot.

4. Add the peppercorns and salt, drizzle with olive oil, cover, then roast gently for 90 minutes.

5. When the beetroot is sticky and soft, remove the skins and roughly chop the flesh. Tip the flesh onto a serving plate and top with rocket, beetroot tops, and the caramelized orange and onion from the tray. Dress with balsamic vinegar, olive oil, dill or fennel fronds, and the reserved orange juice.

Tip
With a glut, batch bake before freezing or pickling for long-term storage.

QUICK MIXED BEETROOT SALAD

A quick and delicious side, this raw, grated salad pairs well with thick slices of goat's cheese and a slice or two of your favourite bread. Packed in a sandwich, it makes the perfect lunch for a day in the garden. If you have a grater attachment for a food processor, this recipe can be made in minutes.

Serves 4

Ingredients

50g (1¾oz) walnuts

1 unwaxed lemon (juice and zest)

1 tsp wholegrain mustard

1½ tbsp extra virgin olive oil

½ tsp white miso

5 or 6 mixed beetroot (purple, golden, and white), scrubbed and grated

2 apples, grated

A bunch of fresh parsley, roughly chopped

1. Toss the walnuts in a pan over a medium heat for 10 minutes to release their aroma. Set aside.

2. Mix the lemon juice and zest with the mustard, olive oil, and miso. Immediately combine with the grated beetroot and apples in a large bowl to stop oxidization (the apples turning brown).

3. Top with the parsley and toasted walnuts.

Radish

Key growing information

- Early spring to late summer
- 1cm (1½in) sowing depth
- 10cm (4in) between plants or clumps
- 4 weeks to harvest
- Full sun
- Half hardy (winter radish is hardy)
- Medium water needs
- Low fertility needs
- 150 plants per sq m
- 3–5kg (6½–11lb) per sq m

Recommended varieties

Summer 'French Breakfast', 'Icicle', 'Scarlet Globe' (pictured right); **Winter** 'Spanish Black Round', 'Daikon'

Growing

The fastest-growing crop of the garden, radish comes in all colours and sizes. Hardier winter radish is an excellent crop to sow late in the season when there are gaps to fill.

STAGE 1

Sowing direct
Sow thinly (every 2–3cm/ ¾–1¼in) in rows 15cm (6in) apart. Cover with soil or compost, and **water** well. There is no need to thin.

Sowing in modules
Multisow 4 or 5 seeds per cell. Cover with soil or compost, and **water** thoroughly. There is no need to thin.

STAGE 2

When sown in modules
Once seedlings have 2 or 3 true leaves, the clumps are ready to **plant out** into their final growing position around 10cm (4in) apart. Create a hole the size of the rootball, press the clump into it, and water well.

Tip
Grow winter radish by sowing in late summer/early autumn in rows either outside or under cover. Thin to 1 plant every 5–7cm (2–3in). Harvest in early winter, or throughout winter if plants are under cover.

STAGE 3

As roots begin to swell, make sure to **water** them well during drier periods to avoid the plants bolting and creating dry, pithy roots.

CONTAINER GROWING

Sow in modules and transplant clumps 10cm (4in) apart. **Water** thoroughly, and harvest when ready.

Cooking

HARVEST
Gently twist and pull roots as needed, selecting the bigger roots first to allow the smaller ones to develop further. Young leaves can also be eaten (best steamed). Leave a few plants to run to seed as radish flowers are not only loved by hoverflies, but are completely edible, along with the green seed pods that follow.

Look out for
Flea beetles may affect direct-sown crops (see p.52).

PICKLED RADISHES
Pickling adds a satisfying acidic crunch to dishes while preserving ingredients in a balanced vinegar liquor. The speed of this process comes from increasing a crop's surface area (by finely chopping or slicing), then submerging it in a pickling liquor of vinegar, sugar, and salt. Do not reuse the liquor for another batch.

If you have a food processor with a blade attachment, this is a lightning-quick recipe. If not, a mandolin is a cheap, fast, and safe way to chop. If you have leftovers like half an onion or carrot, garlic, fresh chilli, apple, herbs, or fennel fronds, add them in.

Makes 2 x 350ml (12fl oz) jars

Ingredients

400ml (14fl oz) apple cider vinegar or white wine vinegar

2 tbsp sugar/honey/maple syrup

1½ tsp sea salt

1 tsp yellow mustard seeds, chilli flakes, star anise, nigella seeds (optional)

300g (10oz) radishes, sliced

1. Heat the vinegar in a small saucepan (with the optional additions if desired) until boiling, then pour it over the sliced vegetables (in a clean, heat-proof jar).

2. Close the lid and let the pickle cool to room temperature. Store at an ambient temperature for 3–6 months until opened, then keep it in a fridge for up to 3 months. Use a fork to lift out the radish.

Meals with ...
Pile the pickled radish into and onto burgers, tacos, salads, sandwiches, broths, or loaded wedges, where their acidity scratches the same itch as ketchup or malt vinegar.

Turnip

Key growing information

- Mid-spring to late summer
- 1cm (½in) sowing depth
- 5–10cm (2–4in) between plants
- 8 weeks to harvest
- Full sun
- Hardy
- Medium water needs
- Medium fertility needs
- 50 plants per sq m
- 7.5kg (16½lb) per sq m

Recommended varieties

'Tokyo Cross' (pictured right), 'Purple Top Milan', 'Golden Ball'

Growing

A fast-growing vegetable, turnip gives you crisp and crunchy roots that can be enjoyed raw or cooked. Easy to grow, it's delicious particularly when small and tender, and has a long sowing season, which is ideal for filling gaps after summer harvests.

STAGE 1
Sowing direct
Use the handle of a rake to make trenches 20cm (8in) apart. **Sow** 1 seed per centimetre.

Sowing in modules
Sow under cover with 4 or 5 seeds per module.

STAGE 2
When sown direct
Thin seedlings to a spacing of 5cm (2in) for smaller roots or 10cm (4in) for larger. Eat the thinnings in a salad.

When sown in modules
Transplant clumps 15cm (6in) apart (pictured above).

STAGE 3
Water turnips well in dry weather to keep a crisp texture and stop them going woody and running to seed.

CONTAINER GROWING
Sow 2 seeds at 5cm (2in) spacing and **thin** to the strongest seedling. Harvest the larger roots first to allow smaller roots to mature.

HARVEST
Harvest the roots when they are golf ball size and larger; you can see the size from what is visible at the surface. The leaves are edible. Later sowings can be overwintered for edible flower shoots in spring. Turnips can be stored in sand (see p.47).

Look out for
Flea beetles make lots of small holes in seedling leaves, particularly in dry spells. To deter them, water seedlings well. If problems persist, start in modules.

Cooking

🔪 VEGETABLE TURNIP HOTPOT

This hearty, comforting dish has a rich vegetable and lentil filling (pictured p.26, centre), topped with golden turnip slices. Potato, parsnip, and swede also work well.

Serves 3

Ingredients

2 tbsp vegetable oil

200g (7oz) chestnut mushrooms, sliced

1 large onion, diced

2 carrots, diced

2 celery sticks, sliced

2 garlic cloves, minced

1 tsp fresh thyme

1 tsp fresh rosemary

1 bay leaf

150g (5½oz) dried green or Puy lentils, rinsed

500ml (16fl oz) vegetable stock

400g (14oz) tin chopped tomatoes

1 tbsp tomato purée

1 tbsp Worcestershire sauce

1 tsp yeast extract

½ tsp freshly ground black pepper

For the topping

1 large or 2 medium turnips, peeled and thinly sliced

1 tbsp olive oil

1 tsp fresh thyme

1. Heat the vegetable oil in a large ovenproof pan over a medium–high heat. Fry the mushrooms for 10 minutes until browned.

2. Lower the heat and add the onion, carrots, and celery for 10 minutes until softened. Add the garlic, thyme, rosemary, and bay leaf, cooking for another minute.

3. Add the lentils, stock, tomatoes, tomato purée, Worcestershire sauce, yeast extract, and black pepper. Simmer for 30 minutes until the lentils are tender and the mixture thickens.

4. Preheat the oven to 190°C (170°C fan/375°F/Gas 5). Arrange the turnip slices in overlapping layers on top of the filling. Brush with olive oil, and season with salt, pepper, and thyme.

5. Bake for 40 minutes until the turnips are golden and tender. Serve hot, ideally with crusty bread or greens.

Celery

Key growing information

- Early spring to early summer
- 0.5cm (1/4in) sowing depth
- 30–35cm (12–14in) between plants
- 16 weeks to harvest
- Partial shade
- Half hardy
- High water needs
- High fertility needs
- 8 plants per sq m
- 4.8kg (10 1/2lb) per sq m

Recommended varieties

'Tall Utah' (pictured right), 'Tango', 'Blush'

Growing

A great plant for shadier spots, celery is a crunchy and aromatic staple for the kitchen – or just to snack on as you potter about the garden. It can be a little trickier to grow than some crops, but give it plenty of water during warm weather and you will be well on the way.

STAGE 1

Sow 2 seeds per module under cover and keep moist. Early sowings will need a heated propagator for germination. **Thin** to the strongest seedling.

STAGE 2

Once seedlings have 3 or 4 true leaves, **pot on** into 7cm (3in) pots and keep them in a frost-protected environment such as a mini-greenhouse.

STAGE 3

Harden off (see p.11) and **transplant** your celery after your last average frost date. **Mulch** with grass clippings, around 5–7cm (2–3in) deep, after transplanting.

Tip

Celery plants must be kept moist to avoid stringy and bitter stems. To ensure this, grow in partial shade to reduce evaporation. In addition to mulching (stage 3), water frequently in the morning during dry weather.

CONTAINER GROWING

Plant 3 celery plants (sown and grown on under cover) equally spaced at 25cm (10in) apart. Keep the container in partial shade and **water** well. **Mulch** with a 2–3cm (1in) layer of grass clippings.

HARVEST

You can either snap off a few stems at a time in a cut-and-

Cooking

Celery is divisive: some love it, some hate it. To me, it's a hero, adding sweet, salty crispness to salads, and wonderful to dip in hummus.

 CELERY AND STILTON SOUP

This recipe will guide you through my process for making blended soups.

Serves 3

Ingredients

1 onion, diced

1 carrot, diced

1 head of celery, diced

2 tbsp olive oil

100ml (3½fl oz) white wine

1 medium waxy potato, peeled and chopped

1 tin haricot or butter beans

1 tsp English mustard

1 litre (1¾ pints) vegetable stock

Ground white pepper

100g (3½oz) Stilton, or 100ml (3½fl oz) coconut milk and 1 tsp white miso

1. Sauté the onion, carrot, and celery in a large pan with olive oil over a medium–low heat for 20 minutes, stirring occasionally. In varying amounts, these ingredients form the base to most soups.

2. Add the wine and let it reduce for 10 minutes, then add everything else except the cheese. Cover and simmer for 40 minutes.

3. Remove the lid and add the cheese.

4. Blend until smooth; serve with crusty bread.

Tip
Try a spoonful or two of parsnip purée as a thickener (see p.43). Stir in just before serving.

Meal prep
This is easy to make in bulk and freeze in portions for up to 1 year. To use, thaw in a fridge and heat until bubbling.

come-again approach, or harvest the entire plant by using a sharp knife to cut the stem just below ground level. Leaves can be used raw in salads or added to soups. To store in a fridge, harvest the whole plant, do not wash it, wrap it in a couple of layers of damp paper towel, and keep in the produce drawer for up to 4 weeks.

Celeriac

Key growing information

- Late winter to early spring
- 0.5cm (1/4in) sowing depth
- 35cm (14in) between plants
- 24 weeks to harvest
- Full sun and partial shade
- Hardy
- High water needs
- High fertility needs
- 9 plants per sq m
- 6kg (13lb) per sq m

Recommended varieties

'Ibis', 'Monarch' (pictured right), 'Giant Prague'

Growing

Also known as celery root, this knobbly root with a subtle, earthy yet sweet and creamy flavour is prized in many restaurants. It enjoys cool climates and provides valuable winter food.

STAGE 1
Sow 2 seeds per module under cover, and place in a heated propagator for germination. **Thin** to the strongest seedling when they've developed their first true leaf.

STAGE 2
When seedlings have developed 3–5 true leaves, **pot on** into 9cm (3 1/2in) pots. Around a week after your last average frost date, **harden off** and transplant.

Tip
For the best results, celeriac needs consistent moisture (see tip, p.54).

STAGE 3
As your plants mature (about 2 months after transplanting), gently snap off the lower leaves around the base to **expose the crown**. This not only helps increase air flow for healthy plants, but also aids the development of the swollen stem, which is the prized harvest!

CONTAINER GROWING
Plant 3 grown-on celeriac plants at equal spacings and maintain a frequent watering regime. Remove lower leaves in mid- to late summer.

HARVEST
From midsummer to early autumn you can take a few leaves for flavouring stocks, soups, and stews, or for a herb salt (see p.166).

Harvest the roots as needed from mid-autumn to early spring by using a fork to gently tease the roots out. The longer the celeriac stands in the ground, the stronger its flavour.

Cooking

🔪 BAKED CELERIAC

Celeriac is one of my favourites, and salt-baked is an absolute classic. For this recipe I'm keeping it simple, celebrating this modest root by pairing it with rocket, lemon, and salt. You can also mix and match with other root veg.

Serves 4

Ingredients

1 garlic bulb

100ml (3½fl oz) extra virgin olive oil

Large pinch of sea salt

2 celeriac, peeled and chopped into large chunks

150g (5½oz) rocket

20g (¾oz) fresh thyme, woody stems removed

80g (2¾oz) extra mature cheese, such as Cheddar or Caerphilly or Emmental, grated

1 unwaxed lemon, zest and juice

Freshly ground black pepper

250g (9oz) butter beans, cooked, drained, and rinsed

1. Preheat the oven to 200°C (180°C fan/400°F/Gas 6).

2. Cut the top 1cm (½in) off the garlic bulb to reveal the cloves, drizzle with some of the olive oil, and add a pinch of salt. Wrap in foil and pop it in the oven for 1 hour.

3. Meanwhile, dress the celeriac with oil and more salt, place on a baking tray, and roast for 50 minutes, tossing halfway through.

4. Add the rocket, thyme, cheese, lemon juice and zest, salt, and pepper to a food processor. Coarsely blend, then add the rest of the olive oil. Squeeze in the garlic and mix.

5. Mix the butter beans with the hot celeriac. Return the tray to the oven for 10 minutes until the beans are starting to split and crack and the celeriac is golden.

6. Serve it dressed with the rocket salsa.

Meal prep
This recipe lends itself to being made ahead of time, portioned, and frozen. To reheat, defrost as many portions as you need in the fridge for 24 hours, then bake at 180°C (160°C fan/350°F/Gas 4) for 25 minutes to reheat.

Fennel

Key growing information

- Mid-spring to midsummer
- 1cm (½in) sowing depth
- 25cm (10in) between plants
- 12 weeks to harvest
- Full sun
- Hardy
- Medium water needs
- Medium fertility needs
- 16 plants per sq m
- 7.2kg (16lb) per sq m

Recommended varieties

'Perfection', 'Rondo' (pictured right), 'Mammoth'

Growing

A beautiful vegetable to look at and eat, fennel is fast-growing and deserves far more attention due to its beautiful fronds (wispy foliage) and the sweet, nutty flavour of the bulb.

STAGE 1
Sowing direct
Sow thinly in rows 25cm (10in) apart, one seed every 2cm (³/₄in). Cover and water.

Sowing in modules
Sow 2 seeds per module tray, keep watered, and **thin** to the strongest.

STAGE 2
When sown direct
Thin seedlings to 1 every 10cm (4in), and thin again a few weeks later to enjoy baby fennel as a harvest.

When sown in modules
Plant out from 2 weeks before the last average frost date, when the seedlings are around 10cm (4in) tall.

STAGE 3
When the bulbous part starts to swell you can **blanch** it by mounding soil up and around the bulb to stop light reaching it, which sweetens its flavour.

CONTAINER GROWING
Sow 2 seeds at 10cm (4in) intervals and **thin** to one seedling. Harvest the largest bulbs first.

HARVEST
Fennel fronds can be picked for salads or teas. Harvest the bulbous part by gripping it and twisting until it releases from the roots. Fennel is best stored in the ground until needed, or in sand (see p.47) for 2–3 months. For two more harvests leave a couple of bulbs in the ground to produce edible flowers and rich aniseed-flavoured green seeds the next year.

Look out for
Fennel is robust, but tends to "bolt" (run to seed early). To prevent this, start it early, choose bolt-resistant types, such as 'Rondo', mulch, and water often.

Cooking

BRAISED FENNEL AND HARICOT CASSEROLE

An elegant and simple casserole, this has layers of aromatics, sweet alliums, and a clean white-wine base. Cooked slowly over a low temperature, these simple ingredients transform in a rich and balanced way. Fennel's powerfully sharp liquorice edge mellows as it's slowly cooked with caramelized notes and a gentle sweetness that infuses the entire dish.

Serves 4

Ingredients
2 fennel bulbs, chopped into a total of 6–8 wedges, fronds removed

2 tbsp olive oil

3 garlic cloves, chopped

1 leek, chopped

1 medium onion, chopped

200ml (7fl oz) white wine

200g (7oz) haricot beans (pre-soaked weight), soaked overnight

1.3 litres (2 pints) stock

½ tsp fennel seeds

Pinch of fresh oregano

4 sage leaves

1. Place a large pot on the stove over a medium heat and leave it to warm for 2–5 minutes.

2. Add the fennel to the pot with the olive oil and let it caramelize on each side for 10 minutes.

3. Add the garlic, leek, and onion to the pot. Cook gently for 15 minutes, stirring occasionally.

4. Add the white wine and let it reduce while you drain the soaked beans.

5. Tip the beans into the pot along with the stock, fennel seeds, oregano, and sage. Reduce the heat, cover, and leave to bubble away for 2 hours.

6. Once the beans are tender, serve with the torn-up fronds on top and a crusty piece of bread.

Tip
To speed up preparation, use 1 drained tin of haricot beans instead of dried.

Fruiting Vegetables

Fruiting Vegetables

Tomato

Key growing information

- Early to mid-spring
- 1cm (½in) sowing depth
- 60cm (24in) between plants
- 16 weeks to harvest
- Full sun
- Tender
- Medium water needs
- High fertility needs
- 3 plants per sq m
- 15kg (33lb) per sq m

Recommended varieties
Cordon 'Tomande' (pictured far right, beefsteak), 'Lulu' (beefsteak), 'Black Russian' (beefsteak), 'Black Strawberry' (cherry), 'Honeycomb' (cherry), 'Tigerella' (pictured centre right, salad), 'Green Zebra' (salad), 'Shimmer' (salad); **Bush** 'Yellow Tumbling Tom' (cherry)

Growing

Can you have a summer without tomatoes? We certainly don't think so! This wonderfully savoury fruit is a garden highlight, perhaps THE garden highlight for some. The moment you taste your first homegrown tomato, you will never look at shop-bought ones in the same way again.

In cooler climates, the best results are grown under cover. But, if you don't have a polytunnel – fear not! There is an increasing choice of productive tomatoes resilient enough to grow outdoors when positioned in the sunniest spot in your garden.

There are two categories of tomatoes: indeterminate (commonly called cordon tomatoes), which tend to be more productive as they continue fruiting until first frost; and determinate (commonly called bush tomatoes), which produce all their fruit in one flush. Most of the tomatoes we grow are cordon as they offer the most variety and greater harvest. Most of the growing information is the same for cordon and bush tomatoes, with the exception of plant supports and pruning.

STAGE 1
Sowing in pots
In early spring, **sow** 1 seed per 7cm (3in) pot of peat-free compost. Use a heated propagator or heat mat for optimal germination with grow lights (see resources, p.216). Keep the compost moist, but never wet.

Once seedlings develop 3–4 true leaves, **pot up** into larger pots, ideally 9cm (3½in) pots to give seedlings extra space to develop roots. The root system has a direct impact on the success of the plant, and we don't want to compromise that early on.

Tomato

When repotting, bury the stem up to the first set of leaves. This corrects any leggy-looking seedlings.

No propagator? No problem!
Wait until mid-spring before sowing and place in a warm spot for germination (an airing cupboard works well). At the first sign of life move the pots to a warm, sunny indoor windowsill. Don't worry if the seedlings start growing towards the light. However, once repotted, rotate your pots 180° daily to maintain an upright habit.

Sowing direct
Every year we allow some self-seeded tomatoes to grow in our polytunnels, and they consistently perform best. This is thanks to them having unrestricted space for early root development. For the same reason, you can **direct sow** tomato seeds in mid-spring in a polytunnel bed, sowing 2 or 3 seeds per hole at 60cm (24in) apart; **water** well. There is a higher risk of a hard late frost compared to when grown in a propagator, so stay vigilant. The short growing season in cooler climates means that the conditions are unsuitable to direct sow tomatoes outdoors.

STAGE 2

When sown in pots
Around a week or two before the last average frost date, **transplant** seedlings under cover. Or wait an additional 2 weeks after that date if planting outdoors for average night-time temperatures to increase. Depending on weather and seedling growth, you may want to **repot** your tomatoes destined for outdoor growing to 2 litre (½ gallon) pots before transplanting, to give them more opportunity to develop.

To **transplant**, dig a hole deep enough to plant the seedling just below the first leaf, and add a 5–7cm (2–3in) layer of compost. Remove the tomato from the pot and place in the hole. Space plants 60cm (24in) apart in rows or plant diagonally to fit more plants per bed.

Water well, about 5 litres (1 gallon) to the base, before backfilling. Firm in, then water again at the base of the stem. Under cover, do not water after the initial transplanting for 4–5 days to encourage downward root growth. Then water well every two days. Outdoors, water whenever there has been no rain for 3–4 days.

Supporting cordon tomatoes under cover
There's no need to support plants for the first 2–3 weeks, to allow seedlings to anchor themselves well. After that point, create a simple vertical support using garden twine and wire. First, run wire horizontally along the top of the polytunnel. Next, loop garden twine around the base of each stem, leaving enough space to fit your thumb through (so as to not choke the plant). Gently spiral the twine around each stem, working up to tie it to the wire overhead. As your plants grow, keep guiding the stems around the twine.

Supporting cordon tomatoes outdoors
Support outdoor cordon tomatoes using stakes or wire cages. You can create a 60cm (24in) diameter cylinder cage using sheets of net-type wire with the 2 long ends tied together. To keep it in place, thread 3 or 4 canes through the wire from the top and push firmly into the ground. The stakes or cage will need to be at least 1.5m (5ft), ideally 1.8m (6ft), tall.

Supporting bush tomatoes
Because a polytunnel is protected from wind, bush tomatoes under cover just need 1 stake around 1.2m (4ft) above ground to tie the plant to. Outdoor bush tomatoes can either be planted with 2 stakes either side as additional support or you can create a 60cm (24in) diameter wire cylinder cage that is staked to the ground and saves you needing to tie the plant to the stake.

STAGE 3
About 4 weeks after transplanting, start to **pinch out** the side shoots of your cordon tomatoes – this is one of Sam's favourite garden jobs! It helps to encourage big fruits and healthy plants. Bush tomatoes are much easier when it comes to pruning: it isn't required.

Tomato

Tip

If you have limited tomato plants, select 1 side shoot towards the base of the stem to train it into a double cordon tomato by giving it its own string support. This essentially gives you 2 plants for 1 – a real winner.

Continue to **water** and consider adding a **mulch** around the base of the plant with a 2–3cm (1in) layer of grass clippings to help retain moisture. When tomato fruits start appearing, **feed** your plants fortnightly with liquid feed (see p.13) to give them additional nutrients. Alternatively, use diluted organic liquid seaweed feed.

6 quickfire tips for tomato success

› Bury stems to first true leaves

› Water regularly

› Support your plants

› Keep on top of pinching out side shoots for cordon tomatoes

› Mulch mature plants

› When fruits appear, feed fortnightly

CONTAINER GROWING

Transplant 1 plant per standard container. Cherry and bush tomatoes are ideal for containers, particularly outside. Place containers against a sunny, sheltered boundary and **support** with a stake or tie against a wall or fence. Container tomatoes need more **water** and additional feed, so it's helpful to **mulch** container tomatoes straight after transplanting to help conserve moisture.

HARVEST

Tomatoes are best enjoyed fully ripe and straight off the vine, ideally warmed by the day's sunshine. Ripe tomato fruits have a little give, similar to a ripe avocado. Do not store your tomatoes in the fridge as it impacts their flavour negatively. Instead, lay them out without overlapping, away from direct sunlight.

Look out for

Tomato fruits crack if watered after the soil has dried out, and inconsistent watering can also cause blossom end rot (see p.69). Tomato blight is a common disease which causes dark lesions on leaves and stems. Remove any signs of blighted material as soon as you spot it, and place on the compost. Maintain good air flow around plant and avoid watering leaves to prevent blight taking hold.

Cooking

One of the best ways to enjoy homegrown tomatoes throughout the season is fresh from the vine, sliced up into a salad or sandwich, topped with extra virgin olive oil, basil, or oregano, and shavings of hard cheese. For a quick snack, we also love grating tomatoes and mixing them with a pinch of salt, olive oil, and crushed garlic. Leave it in the fridge for up to a week and spread over sourdough toast with toppings of your choice.

☐ SKIN-ON TOMATO SAUCE

Nothing beats rustic tomato sauce or any meal made from it. This recipe is designed to take care of your end-of-season fruits, when you need to clear the plants from the garden. Making use of ripe, underripe, and green tomatoes, you'll need roughly six plants to make 10kg (22lb), but the recipe is easily adjusted to your yield. By including the skins, we reduce time and effort and get all that juicy, rich, sweet umami. Best of all, because we grow heirloom varieties, their higher acidity makes them safe to can in a water bath without the need for lemon juice or vinegar, but check using a pH meter to make sure the sauce is below 4.5.

Makes about 12 x 500ml (16fl oz) jars

Ingredients

10kg (22lb) tomatoes, mostly ripe, washed and dried

1–2 tsp sea salt

200ml (7fl oz) water

Equipment

12 x 500ml (16fl oz) glass jars with two-piece lids, sterilized (see p.28)

Jar tongs

Large saucepan

Wire rack or tea towel, to fit in the base of the saucepan

1. Cut off any signs of damage on the tomatoes, then core them, particularly if they are large tomatoes.

2. Chop the tomatoes into chunks and add to a large saucepan with the salt and water. Cook over a medium heat for 2 hours.

3. Once the liquid has reduced by one-third, portion the sauce into the jars, leaving 1cm (½in) beneath the rim.

4. Screw the lids on top, using just your fingertips. This will be tight enough to stop water flooding the sauce during canning, but allow air to escape as it heats.

5. Wash up the saucepan, then set a wire rack or tea towel in the bottom and tightly pack the jars on top. This will stop the jars jostling around or cracking. Fill with enough water to cover the tops of the jars by 3–4cm (1–1½in). Bring to a boil then simmer for 14 minutes.

Tomato

6. Take off the heat, then safely lift the jars from the water using jar tongs. Leave them to cool completely before labelling; the drop in pressure as they cool will seal them. Store in a dark and cool place for up to 12 months.

Alternative recipe

Roast the cored tomatoes for 20 minutes, scorching the skin to release a smoky flavour. You can also add other vegetables (garlic, carrots, celery, etc.) if you want additional flavours or need to bulk out a smaller tomato harvest, but make sure tomatoes are the main ingredient as their acidity is what makes this safe. If you're unsure, freeze the sauce once it's made to halt microbial activity that would otherwise be held back by acid levels.

Meals with...

Once made, your tomato sauce is a potent and healthy ready meal in a jar. Just heat it back up and it's ready to eat. Below are some of my favourite ways to use it in my cooking.

Arrabiata pasta To make this Italian staple, fry off some garlic and dried chillies, then add the sauce to the pan. You can add vegetables and herbs along with your pasta and sauce. You can do the same for bolognese, lasagne, and your favourite pasta bakes.

Pizza Spread your tomato sauce straight from the jar onto a homemade or store-bought pizza base. Top with thick slices of mozzarella and roasted garden vegetables, then cook on your oven's highest setting.

Fisherman's stew Combine sea bass, shrimp, mussels, and clams, and cook in a tomato sauce with garlic, white wine, and mixed vegetables from the garden.

Baked beans Make a batch of baked butterbeans with garlic, onion, carrots, and tomato sauce. Add a dash of soy sauce and smoked paprika, then bake on high until the bean skins split.

Pepper

Key growing information

- Midwinter to early spring
- 0.5cm (¼in) sowing depth
- 40cm (16in) between plants
- 18 weeks to harvest
- Full sun
- Tender
- Medium water needs
- Medium fertility needs
- 6 plants per sq m
- 2.4kg (5¼lb) per sq m

Recommended varieties

Spicy 'Lemon Drop' (pictured far right), 'Tabasco', 'Ring of Fire' (pictured centre right); **Medium** 'Jalapeno'; **Mild** 'Padron' (pictured near right); **Sweet** 'Beauty Bell'

Growing

Also known as capsicum, peppers are a fantastic group of crops, including chillies and bell peppers, that come in many different colours, shapes, and flavour profiles. Chillies contain varying amounts of capsaicin, a source of fiery heat. Bell peppers, on the other hand, contain no, or miniscule, amounts of capsaicin, and so their sweet flavour is at the forefront. All peppers require a long growing season with plenty of heat, so grow under cover for the best results – your efforts will be well rewarded.

STAGE 1
Sow 1 seed per module cell under cover, and place the tray in a heated propagator on a heat mat with a lid on top. Ensure the compost remains moist but not saturated. Use a grow light to help with germination and avoid leggy seedlings.

STAGE 2
When seedlings have 3 or 4 true leaves, **pot** them into 7 or 9cm (3 or 3½in) pots and return them to a bright, warm spot such as a sunny windowsill with a heat mat to continue growing. At this stage, keep the compost on the drier side as pepper seedlings are susceptible to damping off if their feet are too wet; this fungal issue causes them to fall over and wilt very quickly.

STAGE 3
Plant out your peppers into a polytunnel bed or similar once the risk of frost has passed. If you are short on space, consider growing them at the feet of or between cordon tomato plants (see p.62). Watering the tomato plants will provide the soil moisture that peppers need. Otherwise, **water** the peppers whenever the top 7cm (3in) of soil is dry.

CONTAINER GROWING

Transplant 2 grown-on seedlings (stage 2) per container at an equal distance and keep the surface mulched. They will perform best under cover, though may also ripen fruit in a sunny, sheltered spot outside if conditions are consistently warm. You could even grow 1 plant in a 3 litre (2/3 gallon) plant pot on a windowsill that enjoys full sun.

HARVEST

Peppers (both hot and sweet) are ready to harvest when they have turned their desired colour based on the variety, and have some give when squeezed (in comparison with the immature hard fruit).

Carefully cut the fruit away from the plant, keeping 1–2cm (1/2in) of stalk attached. If you have any unripe peppers at the end of the season, place them on a tray inside on a sunny windowsill to encourage them to ripen further.

Tip

If you are after the spiciest chillies, avoid watering the plants once half of the chillies have ripened; this intensifies their heat.

Look out for

Blossom end rot is a physiological disorder caused by inconsistent watering. Water your peppers every couple of days during hot sunny weather, or every 3 days during overcast conditions. Feeding with a natural liquid feed containing calcium may help, too.

Cooking

Peppers are a precious commodity, none more so than chilli peppers. Pick individuals early in the season as they ripen and use chopped up in salads, sandwiches, soups, curries, quick-pickled, blended in hummus, or infused in oil.

HOT SAUCE

At the end of the season you'll likely have a bunch of chillies left at various stages of ripeness, which you can either dehydrate for long-term storage, or ferment into this delicious, complex, beginner-friendly hot sauce. You can make a hot sauce from any and all peppers, sweet or hot. A blend of both actually helps balance your sauce for a more complex, nuanced finish.

The world of hot sauces is vast, with characteristics that range from refreshing citrus to pure liquid fire. Each is expressed further by the living process of fermentation and the wild microbes that you harvest inadvertently along with your chillies.

This recipe's safety relies on using the exact amount of salt in relation to the other ingredients. If you need to adjust it to match your harvest, make sure to add together the weight of all your ingredients, then multiply this total by 0.02. This is the amount of salt you need to use. We haven't given imperial measurements for the ingredients in this recipe as grams offer more accuracy for weighing elements and calculating the safe amount of salt. Fermentation is a living process, and while this recipe is 99% safe, things can go wrong. If you notice a terrible smell or see mould, don't eat it.

Makes 1 x 600ml (1 pint) bottle

Ingredients

150g fresh chillies, roughly chopped, stems removed

350g tomatoes, roughly chopped, stems removed

20g garlic cloves, peeled

20g ginger root, peeled

11g smoked salt

10g fresh sage or oregano

Equipment

Scales

600ml (1 pint) glass clip-top jar, sterilized (see p.28)

600ml (1 pint) glass bottle, sterilized (see p.28)

Glass pebble weight (optional)

Bottle funnel

1. Remove the chilli seeds if you aren't a fan of very hot food. Add all the ingredients into a mixing bowl with the salt and stir.

2. Tip the whole lot into a sterilized glass jar and place the pebble weight on top. Secure the lid and leave it out of direct sunlight at 19–25°C (66–77°F) for 2–3 weeks. During this time you will need to open the jar daily to release the carbon dioxide that builds up. Over time, the tomatoes will release enough liquid to cover the other ingredients and the jar should burst into life with bubbles each time you open it.

3. After 2–3 weeks, tip the fermented sauce into a food processor and blend until smooth. Adjust to taste (perhaps with more aromatics or vinegar), then bottle it and store in a fridge for 1 month to age. You can use it right away, but this ageing process really brings out more of the complexities.

4. Once aged, keep it in the fridge and use it within 6 months.

Tip
If you don't water your chilli and tomato plants for 2 or 3 days prior to harvesting, the sweetness and spice are intensified for this recipe.

Alternative recipe
You can get creative with this recipe by adding a spoonful of homemade jam or rhubarb juice to sweeten it. You can also add citrus, such as lemon or orange, or a handful of rose petals for a floral note. If making these additons, make sure to read the introduction above the main recipe on how to calculate the safe amount of salt to add.

Aubergine

Key growing information

- Late winter to early spring
- 0.5cm (¼in) sowing depth
- 45cm (18in) between plants
- 24 weeks to harvest
- Full sun
- Tender
- Medium water needs
- High fertility needs
- 4 plants per sq m
- 6kg (13lb) per sq m

Recommended varieties

'Black Beauty' (pictured right), 'Long Purple', 'White Dourga'

Growing

Provided you have some under cover space for your aubergines, such as a large cloche or polytunnel, growing them at home is easier than you might think.

STAGE 1

In modules under cover, **sow** 1 seed per cell and place the modules in a bright place on a heat mat or in a propagator to aid germination. **Thin** to the strongest seedling.

STAGE 2

Once seedlings have 2 or 3 true leaves, **pot on** into 9cm (3½in) pots to grow on in a warm place with additional lighting (such as grow lights) to prevent the plants becoming leggy. Keep the compost moist, but do not soak your seedlings.

STAGE 3

Transplant your aubergines around your last average frost date into a cold frame, polytunnel, or similarly protected place. **Feed** your aubergines every 2–3 weeks after planting out.

CONTAINER GROWING

Transplant 1 grown-on aubergine seedling (stage 2) into a container, placing it in a sunny, sheltered position, ideally in a mini-polytunnel or similar. When the plant is around 30cm (1ft) tall, **mulch** at the base to retain moisture.

HARVEST

Aubergines are ripe when the fruits are fully coloured and have some give when squeezed, similar to a ripe mango or avocado. Cut away from the plant with 2–3cm (1in) of stalk attached.

Look out for

Blossom end rot (see p.69) can affect aubergines.

Cooking

MISO AUBERGINE, GREEN BEANS, AND BARLEY

Miso, the deeply umami Japanese bean paste, finds one of its finest partners in aubergine. Its rich, savoury depth soaks into the tender aubergine flesh to create a glaze that's equal parts comfort and indulgence, perfect for a hearty summer dish.

Serves 2–3

Ingredients

100g (3½oz) pearl barley

3 garlic cloves, thinly sliced

100ml (3½fl oz) white wine

700ml (1¼ pints) stock

2 medium-sized aubergines

1 tsp white miso

½ tsp honey or maple syrup

3 tbsp sunflower oil

220g (8oz) green beans, topped and tailod

2 or 3 spring onions, finely chopped

Pickled radish or carrot (optional)

Fresh coriander to garnish

1. Preheat the oven to 200°C (180°C fan/400°F/Gas 6) and toast the barley on a baking tray for 30 minutes, mixing it every 10 minutes.

2. Fry the garlic gently over a low heat for 2–3 minutes.

3. Tip the golden brown toasted barley in with the garlic, white wine, and stock. Cover with a lid and simmer for 30–40 minutes.

4. Remove the top of the aubergines with a sharp knife, then cut in half down the length and score across the flesh in a criss-cross.

5. Bake the aubergine cut side up for 20 minutes, with a small amount of oil rubbed into the open faces. In the meantime mix the miso, honey (or syrup), and a tablespoon of oil.

6. Rub the aubergine with the miso mixture and bake cut side up for a further 25 minutes.

7. Mix the remaining ingredients into the barley broth. The green beans will be blanched in the heat of the broth, and they will be fresh and green. Ladle the broth into serving bowls.

Cucumber

Key growing information

- Mid-spring to early summer
- 0.5cm (¼in) sowing depth
- 50cm (20in) between plants
- 14 weeks to harvest
- Full sun
- Tender
- High water needs
- High fertility needs
- 4 plants per sq m
- 12kg (26½lb) per sq m

Recommended varieties

Outdoor growing 'Marketmore' (pictured far right);
Indoor growing 'Tanja', 'Passandra' (pictured right)

Growing

The first time you taste a homegrown cucumber you'll realize just how delicious these watery fruits can be! With abundant harvests that can outperform courgettes (which are notorious for their gluts), they are a must-grow. Cucumber varieties are bred specifically to be grown indoors or outdoors, so it's essential to choose one that fits your situation.

STAGE 1

Sow 1 seed per 7cm (3in) pot in a warm and bright place such as an outdoor mini-greenhouse or inside a polytunnel; this helps with germination. On particularly cold nights you may need to **protect** the plants as they aren't frost hardy. Either bring them indoors or cover them in fleece for insulation (see p.11).

STAGE 2

Once the risk of frost has passed, and seedlings have 4 or 5 true leaves, it is time to plant out. **Harden off** the plants if they're going to be grown outdoors (see p.11). Both indoors and out, create a hole larger than the rootball for each plant, adding a generous handful of compost at the base. **Plant** and firm the cucumber, then **water** in.

STAGE 3

A couple of weeks after planting out, create a **support** structure if you want to maximize yield per square metre, and to grow the best quality fruits that aren't lying on the ground. We've found that the simplest way to **train** cucumbers is to create a pyramid structure using 4 sticks each about 1.5m (5ft) long, buried 30cm (1ft) into the ground. Place 1 stick on the inside of each of the

Cucumber

4 plants in a square metre, and tie the 4 sticks together as a pyramid. Wrap string around the whole structure to create a climbing frame for the cucumbers. **Water** the plants consistently and **prune** any branches that grow away from the structure, or gently tie them back into place.

CONTAINER GROWING

After hardening off (stage 2), **plant** 2 cucumbers per container. Encourage them to grow up inside a simple vertical structure such as 3 1.5m (5ft) lengths of bamboo buried into the pot around the edge and tied together at the top; wrap string in a spiral up the structure. Keep them well watered.

HARVEST

The fruits are ready to harvest when they are dark green and firm, and at a desired size (though at least 10cm (4in) long). Make sure you pick them before the skin starts to turn yellow as the colour change is a sign of increased bitterness.

Look out for

Powdery mildew is a fungal disease that makes your plant look as if white flour has been shaken over the leaves. Avoid it by ensuring good air flow around your plants, and watering at the base of the plant rather than on the leaves. Stay vigilant and remove any affected leaves if necessary.

Cooking

Cucumbers are versatile and can be added to many recipes. Try them grated into Greek yoghurt with lemon juice and dill for tzatziki; sliced into a soft goat's cheese and lettuce sandwich; chopped roughly and dressed with soy sauce, toasted sesame oil, and sesame seeds for a savoury salad; or chilled with yoghurt, mint, and a pinch of salt to make a cold soup starter. Add slices into cold water with a wedge of lemon for a refreshing drink.

QUICK PICKLED CUCUMBER SALAD

This crisp, refreshing salad includes lightly pickled cucumbers, fresh herbs, and borage flowers.

Serves 2

Ingredients

1 large cucumber, thinly sliced

Pinch of sea salt

2 tbsp white wine vinegar or apple cider vinegar

1 tsp sugar

1 tbsp extra virgin olive oil

1 small shallot, finely sliced

1 handful of radishes, thinly sliced

1 tbsp fresh dill, chopped

1 tbsp fresh mint, chopped

1 tsp zest of an unwaxed lemon

Freshly ground black pepper

Borage flowers, to garnish (optional)

1. Place the cucumber slices in a bowl, sprinkle with salt, and toss. Let them sit for 10 minutes to draw out excess moisture, then drain.

2. In a small bowl, whisk the vinegar, sugar, and olive oil. Stir in the shallot and cucumber and let it sit for 30 minutes to soften.

3. Combine with the radishes, dill, mint, and lemon zest in a serving bowl.

4. Season with black pepper and scatter the borage flowers on top. Serve at once or chill for up to 24 hours ahead of time.

Meals with …

Here are a couple of ideas for this pickled salad.

Sandwich filling Add along with cheese or fish.

Burger topping Place on top of a burger patty, where the acidity balances the rich, fatty umami of the burger.

Cucumber

SUNOMONO SALAD

This light, refreshing Japanese cucumber salad offers a delicate balance of sweet and savoury flavours. It is great as a topping for light or meaty clear broths or as a side to main meals. *Sunomono* (酢の物) literally means "vinegared things" in Japanese.

Ingredients
1 large cucumber, thinly sliced

½ tsp sea salt

2 tbsp rice vinegar

1 tsp sugar

½ tsp soy sauce

½ tsp sesame oil

4–5 wakame seaweed strands, thinly sliced (rehydrated, optional)

1 tbsp sesame seeds, toasted

1 tbsp spring onions, thinly sliced

1. Place the cucumber slices in a bowl, sprinkle with salt, and toss gently. Let them sit for 10 minutes to draw out excess moisture. Rinse under cold water, drain well, and squeeze lightly to remove excess liquid.

2. In a small bowl, whisk the rice vinegar, sugar, soy sauce, and sesame oil until the sugar dissolves.

3. Combine the cucumber and wakame in a bowl, pour over the dressing, and toss to coat. Refrigerate for at least 1 hour.

4. Sprinkle with toasted sesame seeds and spring onions. Serve chilled for the best flavour.

Courgette

Key growing information

- Mid-spring to early summer
- 0.5cm (¼in) sowing depth
- 1m (3ft) between plants
- 12 weeks to harvest
- Full sun
- Tender
- High water needs
- High fertility needs
- 1 plant per sq m
- 6kg (13lb) per sq m

Recommended varieties

'Black Beauty' (pictured right, dark green), 'Romanesco' (light green), 'Shooting Star' (yellow), 'Tondo Di Nizza' (round), 'Black Forest' (climbing)

Growing

Courgettes are one of the fastest-growing and most productive crops you can grow – 2 plants will usually be ample for a hungry family! With a range of interesting varieties (and colours) to choose from, and uses in the kitchen, they are seeing a well-deserved comeback in popularity.

STAGE 1

Sow 1 seed per 9cm (3½in) pot under cover. Courgettes need a little warmth to germinate and so early sowings will benefit from the use of a heat mat or propagator.

STAGE 2

Once the seeds have germinated, move them into a polytunnel or mini-greenhouse if they've been on your indoor windowsill. Ensure you **protect** the plants on cold nights (see p.11).

STAGE 3

If you are planting out around your last average frost date, **harden off** your courgettes first (see p.11). Otherwise **plant** them straight out in their final growing position. Make a hole slightly larger than the rootball and add a healthy handful of compost to the base of the hole to support their need for fertility – and ultimately, their abundance.

CONTAINER GROWING

Transplant 1 grown-on courgette seedling (stage 3) per container. You can plant trailing courgette plants in containers to climb up fences or trellises to maximize vertical space and yield; the variety 'Black Forest' is particularly

suitable for this, making it perfect for balcony or patio gardens.

HARVEST

It comes down to personal preference as to when to harvest courgettes. You may like to eat them as baby fruits, only 10cm (4in) long, or you might prefer marrows (courgettes allowed to grow huge). Whatever stage you harvest, use a sharp knife to cut the courgette away from the plant (pictured above) with around 5cm (2in) of stem attached if you need to store them for a few weeks.

Look out for
Fruit rot is very similar to blossom end rot (see p.69), but is usually caused by weather and pollination issues rather than inconsistent soil moisture. If a female courgette flower has not been pollinated, the fruit will begin forming but will then die off. Prevent this by growing at least 2 plants in close proximity to increase the chances of multiple male flowers nearby. Long periods of cool weather can also cause fruit rot; just remain patient until it brightens up – you'll soon be inundated. Powdery mildew can also affect courgette plants (see p.75).

Cooking

Courgettes are a favourite summer crop, with endless ways to cook and preserve them – which is handy, as you'll quickly find yourself harvesting daily just to keep on top of them. Butter soft, and delicious charred, courgettes can be used as a centrepiece (see carpaccio) or hidden in recipes to help add bulk (see lentil burger).

COURGETTE CARPACCIO

This is a crisp, refreshing summer salad.

Serves 2

Ingredients

1 medium courgette, very thinly sliced

2 tbsp extra virgin olive oil

1 unwaxed lemon, juice and zest

½ tsp flaky sea salt

¼ tsp freshly ground black pepper

1 tbsp chopped fresh basil or mint

1 tbsp toasted pine nuts (or pistachios or sunflower seeds)

20g (¾oz) crumbled feta or shaved Parmesan

Nasturtium flowers and leaves to garnish (optional)

1. Use a mandolin or sharp knife to slice the courgette into thin rounds. Arrange them in a single layer on a serving plate.

2. Whisk together the olive oil, lemon juice, lemon zest, salt, and pepper.

3. Drizzle the dressing over the courgette slices so they are well coated. Sprinkle with chopped herbs, toasted pine nuts (or sunflower seeds or pistachios), and feta (or Parmesan).

4. Let it sit for 10 minutes before serving to allow the flavours to meld, then scatter with nasturtium flowers and leaves (if using).

COURGETTE AND LENTIL BURGER

This hearty lentil burger, too fragile to barbecue, is an ideal hot summer lunch. It's spiced with ras el hanout, a North African blend that translates to "head of the shop": the best the spice merchant has to offer. Its flavour is warm, complex, aromatic, and subtly sweet, with a bit of earthy heat.

Serves 6

Ingredients
For the patties

1 small onion, diced

250g (9oz) mushrooms (oyster or chestnut)

1 large courgette, chopped

2 garlic cloves, peeled

Olive oil, to drizzle

2 tbsp ras el hanout

½ tsp fresh oregano

90g (3oz) rolled oats

200g (7oz) speckled lentils, soaked and cooked in vegetable stock

1 tbsp soy sauce

1 tsp Worcestershire sauce

30g (1oz) gordal olives, pitted

1 tsp sesame seeds

To serve
Cheese, sliced

6 tbsp mayonnaise

1 tsp wholegrain mustard

6 burger buns

Fresh tomato, sliced

A few fresh lettuce leaves

Pickled vegetables, kimchi (see p.108), or sauerkraut

1. Lightly pulse the onion, mushrooms, courgette, and garlic in a food processor to form a coarse paste in which there are visible pieces of the vegetables.

2. Add a drizzle of olive oil to a large frying pan, then fry the vegetables for 15 minutes, adding the spice and oregano after 5 minutes.

3. Preheat the oven to 200°C (180°C fan/400°F/Gas 6), and line a baking tray with parchment.

4. Blend the oats into a coarse flour, then add the fried vegetables and all the remaining patty ingredients and pulse a few times to bring the mixture together.

5. Shape the mixture into 6 even balls, then press each into a patty. If the mixture is too sticky, use oil on your hands.

6. Lay the patties on the tray and bake for 15–20 minutes. After 10 minutes, place a slice of cheese on top of each patty to melt.

7. While they bake, mix the mayonnaise and mustard together. Load up the burger buns with slices of tomato, the mayo-mustard mix, and lettuce.

8. Finally, assemble the burgers with a handful of homemade pickles, kimchi, or sauerkraut and tuck in.

Meal prep
To freeze your burgers, after step 5, layer the patties with parchment and freeze in an airtight container for up to 9 months. To cook, defrost in the fridge overnight and bake for 25–30 minutes until the burgers are golden brown.

Winter Squash

Key growing information

- Mid-spring to early summer
- 0.5cm (¼in) sowing depth
- 1–2m (3–6ft) between plants
- 18 weeks to harvest
- Full sun
- Tender
- High water needs
- High fertility needs
- 1 plant per sq m (but ideally 2sq m per plant)
- 6kg (13lb) per sq m

Recommended varieties

'Crown Prince', 'Jumbo Pink Banana', 'Uchiki Kuri' (pictured right), 'Jack-o-Lantern' (pumpkin), spaghetti squash

Growing

Known as winter squash thanks to their fantastic storage capabilities, this group of squash is one of our favourite crops to grow in abundance in the garden. With so many fascinating varieties and types to choose from beyond the pumpkin, all with their own unique shape and flavour, it's hard to ever get bored growing winter squash.

STAGE 1

Sow 1 seed in a 9cm (3½in) pot under cover. Early sowings benefit from a heat mat or propagator to aid germination; place on a polytunnel bench or sunny indoor windowsill. Later sowings (after your last average frost date) can be in a polytunnel with no heat.

STAGE 2

Once the seed has germinated, **grow on** in a polytunnel or cold frame until it has 7 or 8 true leaves.

STAGE 3

Prepare the final growing position by digging a 30 x 30cm (12 x 12in) hole and mixing in a couple of shovels of compost. **Plant** each squash plant and **water** in generously.

CONTAINER GROWING

Plant 1 winter squash seedling (stage 3) per container. **Feed** (see p.13) every couple of weeks from midsummer onwards with liquid feed to fuel their prolonged growth and high fertility needs.

HARVEST

Winter squash is typically harvested around the first frost. Harvest using a sharp knife or pair of secateurs. Cut the fruit from the vine with at least a 5cm (2in) stump, but preferably 10cm (4in), for the best storage results over winter.

Look out for

Powdery mildew (see p.75) and fruit rot (see p.79) may affect winter squash.

Cooking

WINTER SQUASH AND GOAT'S CHEESE GALETTE

This golden, flaky galette is the perfect autumnal feast.

Serves 2–3

Ingredients
For the pastry

100g (3½oz) cold unsalted butter, cubed

200g (7oz) plain flour

½ tsp sea salt

1 tsp chopped fresh oregano

3 tbsp cold milk

For the filling

400g (14oz) winter squash, peeled and thinly sliced

1 tbsp olive oil, plus more to finish

½ tsp sea salt

¼ tsp freshly ground black pepper

1 tbsp butter

1 small onion, thinly sliced

100g (3½oz) soft goat's cheese, crumbled

1 tbsp honey

1 tsp chopped fresh oregano

To finish

1 small egg, beaten (for glazing)

1 tsp sesame seeds (optional)

Large pinch of flaky sea salt

1. First make the pastry. Rub butter, flour, and salt together until they have a breadcrumb-like texture. Stir in the oregano, then gradually add cold milk until a dough forms. Cover and chill for 30 minutes.

2. Preheat the oven to 200°C (180°C fan/400°F/Gas 6). Toss the squash with olive oil, salt, and pepper, then roast for 20 minutes until it's tender when tested.

3. Melt the butter over a low heat, add the onions, and cook for 15 minutes, stirring until caramelized.

4. Roll out the pastry to about 3mm (⅛in) thick and lay it on a lined tray. Layer squash, onions, and goat's cheese in the centre, leaving a 5cm (2in) border. Drizzle with honey and olive oil, then sprinkle with oregano.

5. Fold in the edges, brush with egg wash, and sprinkle with sesame seeds and flaky sea salt. Bake for 30–35 minutes until golden.

Fruiting Vegetables

Sweetcorn

Key growing information

- Mid- to late spring
- 1cm (½in) sowing depth
- 35cm (14in) between plants
- 16 weeks to harvest
- Full sun
- Tender
- Medium water needs
- Medium fertility needs
- 8–10 plants per sq m
- 3kg (7lb) per sq m

Recommended varieties

'Golden Bantam', 'Earlibird' (pictured right), 'Early Damuan'

Growing

A much-loved vegetable, sweetcorn creates height in the garden. Try your first cob raw – so sweet and creamy!

STAGE 1

Sow 1 seed per module cell and place in a warm area such as a mini-greenhouse to help germination.

STAGE 2

When seedlings are around 10cm (4in) in height they are ready to transplant. **Plant out** sweetcorn in a grid pattern, such as 4 x 4, with at least 16 plants. This will ensure successful wind pollination and sweetcorn formation. Fewer plants will lead to poor yields.

STAGE 3

Once the plants are at least 45cm (18in) tall, **mulch** the ground with a 5cm (2in) layer of grass clippings or straw to retain moisture in the soil.

CONTAINER GROWING

Sweetcorn is generally not suitable for growing in containers unless you grow 2 plants per container (planted out when seedlings are 10cm (4in) tall) and have at least 8 containers together in a "block" formation.

HARVEST

Sweetcorn is ready to harvest when the "silks" at the top of the corn turn dark brown and dry. Another sign is if you gently open up a cob and pierce a kernel, it should exude a milky liquid. To pick, snap the sweetcorn downwards and away from the plant.

Look out for

Rodents such as mice and voles can sometimes target ripe cobs, so avoid leaving these cobs on the plant for more than a couple of days.

Sweetcorn

Cooking

BARBECUED SWEETCORN WITH BLACKCURRANT

This smoky, buttery corn on the cob is elevated with tangy-savoury blackcurrant (see p.192), which adds a burst of umami and brightness. It's delicious with grilled vegetables, tofu skewers, or a crisp summer salad as part of a summer picnic feast.

Serves 4

Ingredients

4 fresh corn on the cob, husks removed

1 tbsp olive oil

2 tbsp unsalted butter, softened

½ tsp flaky sea salt (optional)

For the blackcurrant glaze

2 tbsp brine left over from blackcurrant boshi (see p.192)

1 tbsp mirin

1 tbsp soy sauce

1 tsp honey or maple syrup

½ tsp grated fresh ginger

1. In a small pan over a low heat, combine the blackcurrant brine, mirin, soy sauce, honey, and ginger. Simmer for 1–2 minutes until slightly thickened. Set aside.

2. Prepare the barbecue embers for a medium–high heat. Leave the corn whole or, if it's already naked, brush with olive oil and place it directly on the grill. Keep them piping hot and turn every 5–10 minutes. Cook for 15–30 minutes.

3. Spread unsalted butter over the hot corn, then brush generously with the blackcurrant mixture. Sprinkle with sea salt, if needed, and enjoy warm.

Alliums

Leek

Key growing information

- Mid- to late spring
- 1cm (½in) sowing depth
- 20cm (8in) between plants
- 24 weeks to harvest
- Full sun
- Hardy
- Medium water needs
- Medium fertility needs
- 25 plants per sq m
- 9kg (20lb) per sq m

Recommended varieties

'Musselburgh' (pictured right), 'Bandit', 'Blue Solaise'

Growing

Our favourite of the winter crops, leeks offer great versatility in the kitchen and are packed with flavour. While they need a long growing season to develop, they are worth waiting for.

STAGE 1

Use a rake handle to create a 1cm (½in) deep trench in a bed. Space rows about 15cm (6in) apart if you are growing lots of leeks. Then thickly **sow** 2 or 3 seeds per centimetre, cover over, and keep well watered. Every 10cm (4in) should produce around 10 seedlings.

STAGE 2

When the seedlings are around pencil thickness, use a fork to gently lift them and place them in a bucket of water. Gently separate the seedlings, removing the small ones.

Plant out using a large dibber to make holes 15cm (6in) deep, and drop a seedling into each hole; the top of each will stick out above the ground. **Water** in for 3 seconds. Do not fill the hole with soil as the water will move enough soil to cover the roots, and the remaining hole will provide space to help the leeks swell in size. For the smaller seedlings, pot them up with 10 seedlings per 17cm (7in) pot. These can be back-ups, or treated like a spring onion. Alternatively, compost them.

STAGE 3

A month after transplanting, **mulch** around the base of your leeks with grass, straw, or similar. This will retain moisture and suppress weeds and provides a slow release of fertility during the long growing season.

CONTAINER GROWING

Sow a group of 3 seeds at a spacing of 15cm (6in) between each group. After

Leek

germination, **thin** to the largest and allow it to grow on. **Water** well and **mulch** the leeks when the seedlings are around 20cm (8in) tall.

HARVEST

Harvest leeks from early winter onwards, selecting the largest ones to allow the smaller ones to continue maturing. Depending on soil conditions, you can either pull out the whole leek, or, if there is strong resistance, push a fork down into the soil 10cm (4in) from the stem and then push the fork downwards while pulling the leek upwards to prise it out from the ground. Before storing, peel off the outer layer of leek leaves, and thoroughly wash the roots.

Tip
Consider leaving a handful of plants in the ground in spring to allow them to flower. Leek flowers can not only be pickled or added to salads, but they are one of the best flowers for attracting bumblebees and butterflies to the garden (pictured above right).

Look out for
The larvae of leek moth, also known as onion leaf miner, burrows into the stems of leeks. Prevent this by using pheromone traps, or growing leeks under insect mesh. Leeks can also be affected by rust (see p.97), though they tend to shake off rust over winter, so be patient if it appears on plants in autumn.

Cooking

As sweet as shallots, as aromatic as garlic, and as fundamental as onions, leeks are the hero of Welsh cuisine and a criminally underappreciated member of the allium family.

BRAISED LEEKS AND BUTTER BEANS

A rich, comforting dish of slow-braised leeks and tender butter beans, this is lifted with white wine, wholegrain mustard, and fresh parsley.

Serves 2

Ingredients

2 tbsp olive oil

1 tbsp butter

2 large leeks, cut into 10cm (4in) pieces

2 garlic cloves, finely chopped

100ml ($3^{1}/_{2}$fl oz) dry white wine

400g (14oz) tin of butter beans, drained and rinsed

300ml (10fl oz) vegetable stock

1 tbsp wholegrain mustard

1 tsp pickled green peppercorns

$1/2$ tsp sea salt

$1/4$ tsp freshly ground black pepper

100ml ($3^{1}/_{2}$fl oz) double cream

2 tbsp fresh parsley, chopped

Toasted walnuts, to finish (optional)

1. Heat the olive oil and butter in a large pan over a medium heat. Add the leeks and cook for 10 minutes, turning them until golden all the way round. Remove and set aside.

2. In the same pan, sauté the garlic until softened and aromatic.

3. Pour in the white wine and let it bubble until reduced by half. Stir in the butter beans, stock, mustard, peppercorns, salt, and pepper. Nestle the leeks back into the pan.

4. Cover and simmer gently for 25–30 minutes, until the leeks are soft.

5. Stir through the cream and half the parsley. Taste and adjust seasoning if needed.

6. Serve warm, scattered with the remaining parsley (and toasted walnuts, if using), with plenty of crusty bread to mop up the sauce.

Tip
For extra indulgence, melt some thyme compound butter (see p.164) or regular butter at the end before adding the cream.

Leek

Onion

Key growing information

- Early to mid-spring
- 1cm (½in) sowing depth
- 15cm (6in) between plants
- 24 weeks to harvest
- Full sun
- Hardy
- Medium water needs
- Medium fertility needs
- 35 plants per sq m
- 12kg (26½lb) per sq m

Recommended varieties

White 'Albion'; **Yellow** 'Ailsa Craig'; **Red** 'Red Baron';
To grow from sets 'Sturon' (pictured right and far right)

Growing

A staple in both the garden and the kitchen, with many different varieties to choose from, onions are a low-effort crop that delivers flavour and yield. For how to grow onions from sets, see right.

STAGE 1
Sowing in modules
Sow 2 seeds per module cell and keep in a warm spot to aid germination. Keep the soil moist but not wet and, once germinated, **thin** to one seedling per cell.

STAGE 2
Transplant seedlings when they reach 10cm (4in) tall. If the days are cold, **harden them off** before transplanting (see p.11). Remove each seedling from its cell and use a trowel to make a hole a little deeper than the rootball. Place the rootball in the hole, firm it in, and press down the surrounding soil to create a natural dip around the seedling – this makes watering more efficient. **Water** well.

STAGE 3
Once plants are 30cm (12in) tall, **mulch** them with a thin layer of grass clippings (2–3cm/1in). This is to retain moisture in the soil to help the bulbs swell and reduce the chance of plants running to seed, thus lowering yield. Continue to **water** plants well during dry periods.

GROWING FROM SETS
Onion sets are immature bulbs that can be planted and then mature to full size. While they are more expensive than seed, they are still much cheaper than buying onions from the shop, and this is our preferred method. They are a great time saver as you don't need to worry about germination or thinning. **Plant** one per module at half the bulb's depth. **Transplant** each one at 15cm (6in) tall, spacing them 15cm (6in) apart.

CONTAINER GROWING

If you are growing onions only in containers then consider buying a bag of onion sets to reduce the space needed for module sowings. **Plant** sets directly in the container in mid-spring, spaced 15cm (6in) apart, at half their depth in the soil. **Water** and **mulch** the plants well with grass clippings or straw.

HARVEST

Harvest onion leaves as needed, taking only one from each plant at a time. Onion bulbs are ready to harvest when the green tops begin to flop over (pictured above). Pick by twisting and pulling the tops to release the bulbs.

Look out for

Onion flies burrow into the bulbs of onions, causing them to rot and the leaves to wilt and turn yellow. These can be avoided or reduced by growing under mesh, planting out onions in late spring, or growing from sets. Onions are also affected by onion leaf miner (see p.89).

Cooking

Onions are one of the foundational aromatic ingredients, along with peppers, carrots, celery, and garlic. Their sweet flavour and rich fragrance make a strong base to most meals, so grow plenty.

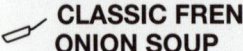 CLASSIC FRENCH ONION SOUP

A rich French onion soup is a thing to behold, made with slow-caramelized homegrown onions and topped with crisp croutons and melted cheese. It's perfect for a cosy evening after a long Sunday in the garden.

Serves 3–4

Ingredients
For the soup
40g (1½oz) unsalted butter

1 tbsp olive oil

1kg (2¼lb) onions, peeled and thinly sliced (see tip)

2 garlic cloves, finely chopped

1 tsp sea salt

½ tsp freshly ground black pepper

2 tbsp plain flour

200ml (7fl oz) dry white wine

1.2 litres (2 pints) beef or vegetable stock

2 sprigs fresh thyme

1 bay leaf

1 tsp Worcestershire sauce (optional)

For the croutons
1 small baguette or sourdough loaf, sliced

1 tbsp olive oil

1 garlic clove, peeled and halved

To finish
150g (5½oz) Gruyère cheese, grated (or Comté for a stronger flavour)

50g (1¾oz) Parmesan, grated

1. In a large, heavy-bottomed pan, melt the butter with the olive oil over a low heat. Add the onions, garlic, salt, and pepper. Cook slowly, stirring occasionally, for 50 minutes to an hour until the onions turn deep golden brown.

2. Stir in the flour and cook for 2 minutes to remove the raw taste of the flour. Pour in the white wine and scrape up any caramelization from the pan. Simmer until the wine reduces by half.

3. Add the stock, thyme, and bay leaf. Bring to a simmer, then cover and cook on a low heat for 30 minutes.

4. Meanwhile, preheat the oven to 180°C (160°C fan/350°F/Gas 4) for the croutons. Brush the bread slices with olive oil and bake for 15–20 minutes until crisp. Rub the crispy toast with the cut garlic clove while still warm.

5. Stir in the Worcestershire sauce to the soup, if using, remove the thyme and bay leaf, and adjust the seasoning if needed.

6. Ladle the hot soup into ovenproof bowls, top with croutons, and sprinkle generously with Gruyère and Parmesan. Grill for 5 minutes until the cheese is golden and bubbling.

Tip
If using freshly harvested onions, reserve the undamaged tops and thinly slice them to sprinkle on the cheese before serving to reintroduce a fresh, lively onion flavour to the dish.

Alliums

Garlic

Key growing information

- Mid- to late autumn
- 5cm (2in) planting depth
- 15cm (6in) between plants
- 32 weeks to harvest
- Full sun
- Hardy
- Medium water needs
- Medium fertility needs
- 30 plants per sq m
- Yield per sq m 2.5kg (5½lb)

Recommended varieties

Hardneck 'Kingsland Wight', 'Caulk Wight', 'Carcassonne Wight' (pictured far right); **Softneck** 'Solent Wight'

Growing

There are two types of garlic: hardneck and softneck. We recommend hardneck garlic as it is the most hardy and reliable for gardeners; it also produces larger cloves with more complex flavours. However, if you need a crop for longer storage, softneck will store for up to twice as long as hardneck (though you can preserve garlic in other ways, see pp.210–211).

STAGE 1
Plant individual garlic cloves by pushing them into the soil with the pointier end facing upwards. Cover the hole over with soil. There is no need to water them in.

STAGE 2
Shoots should start emerging in early winter. There is no need to protect the plants as they slowly grow through winter. When the plants are around 20cm (8in) tall you can **mulch** them with leaves, straw, or grass to retain moisture during early spring and reduce pressure from weeds.

STAGE 3
Hardneck garlic sends up shoots called scapes around mid-spring. Give these 3 days to grow and then snap them off from where they emerge to divert energy towards bulb development rather than producing flowers, and then seeds. These scapes are delicious to eat (see p.99).

CONTAINER GROWING
Plant garlic at a spacing of 15cm (6in) between each clove. **Mulch** when the shoots appear. Due to the timing of its growing cycle, garlic is a great way to use containers over the winter months after your summer harvests.

HARVEST
From mid-spring you can harvest green garlic for its stem and immature bulb. Peel and compost the outer

Garlic

two layers of the stem before using the rest in cooking (see p.98). Opt for the thickest stems for green garlic – at least 2.5cm (1in) in diameter. You can also harvest scapes, as in stage 3.

For mature bulbs, harvest in early summer, when the bottom half of the leaves has turned yellow. If you are struggling to pull out the plants, use a hand fork to gently prise the bulbs from the ground.

Look out for
Rust is a fungal disease that reduces the yield and vigour of garlic and other alliums. It is easy to recognize as you see rusty-orange spots appearing on leaves. The best way to slow its spread is to cut out impacted leaves. When rust occurs close to harvest time, it can be left alone as it will have little impact on harvest.

Cooking

GARLIC IN THE KITCHEN

One of the most versatile aromatics in our kitchen, garlic provides depth, sweetness, and pungency to dishes. It is used in many recipes to build a well-rounded, delicious base. Add it when sautéing vegetables for any dinner, sauce, dip, or dressing for a punchy kick, or slowly roast or confit (cook slowly in fat) for a soft, mellow, buttery version. Fry until golden brown for crispy garlic slices that can be stored in an airtight container and sprinkled over dishes, or crush cloves into butter with parsley for the best garlic bread in the world.

What a lot of people don't realize until they grow their own garlic is just how many culinary offerings the plant has in addition to the widely used mature, cured bulb.

Green garlic

Garlic harvested before individual cloves form is called green garlic (pictured left), and resembles a young leek. The entire plant is edible, sweet, and very juicy, lending itself to dishes as a delicate alternative to leek or garlic.

Wet garlic

Freshly harvested, fully developed garlic bulbs are the gold standard for chefs all over the world. What you're likely to find in supermarkets is cured garlic (pictured bottom right), which has been hung to dry for long-term storage. Wet garlic drips with pungent, delicious juices that weave their way through your meal and infuse it like no other garlic harvest can. Use it as you would cured garlic, but cherish every mouthful.

Cured garlic

Clean the harvested garlic (the whole plant, root to leaf) and hang in a well-ventilated space, either plaiting plants together using their tops, or placing them over a rack or mesh. It's important not to overcrowd them or they could go mouldy. Leave them to cure out of direct sunlight for 2–4 weeks before trimming off the papery dead leaves and storing the bulbs in a cloth bag, wooden crate, or hung braided in the kitchen (at or below 18°C/64°F). Softneck varieties last 9–12 months, while hardneck varieties last 3–6 months.

Scapes

These tall pre-flowering spires (pictured top right) appear in spring. You'll want to snap them off as soon as they appear to encourage a sweet, fat bulb. Firm in texture and delicious in taste, they can be charred, blended with olive oil, and used as a dressing for salad, pasta, or pizza.

Flowers

If you miss a scape and it starts to flower, pick the delicate white flowers and use them as a garnish for salads and soups.

Tops

When harvesting garlic bulbs, remove some of the healthy green leaves and blend them into sauces, soups, and hummus. You can also chop them up and add them into tortilla and omelettes right at the end of cooking, allowing the residual heat to steam them and release their aroma.

Spring Onion

Key growing information

- Early spring to midsummer
- 1cm (½in) sowing depth
- 10cm (4in) between clumps of plants
- 12 weeks to harvest
- Full sun
- Hardy
- Medium water needs
- Medium fertility needs
- 500 plants per sq m
- 8kg (18lb) per sq m

Recommended varieties

'Ishikura', 'Lilia' (pictured right), 'North Holland Blood Red', 'White Lisbon'

Growing

Fast growing and excellent for filling gaps later in the growing season, spring onions add so much flavour to salads and are a great finishing garnish.

STAGE 1
In modules **sow** 8–10 seeds per cell and place in a warm area under cover or on an indoor windowsill to germinate. Keep the compost moist but not wet to avoid seed rot.

STAGE 2
Once seedlings appear, move the module tray into a bright but cooler space under cover, such as a mini-greenhouse, cold frame, or polytunnel.

STAGE 3
Plant out when seedlings are 7–10cm (3–4in) tall. Make a hole using a trowel and place a clump in the hole, pressing down firmly and watering in. Do not separate the seedlings in the clump; they will all grow together.

CONTAINER GROWING
Spring onions work well in containers due to their compact habit. Start off under cover in modules as in stages 1 and 2. **Plant** clumps of seedlings 10cm (4in) apart.

HARVEST
Pick spring onions when they are at your desired size, carefully twisting and pulling the biggest plant from the clump to allow the others to continue growing.

Look out for
Onion fly (see p.93) affects spring onions, though it's much less severe and common than on onions.

Cooking

🔪 SPRING ONION FRITTERS

These golden, crispy fritters are packed with the sweet, mild bite of spring onions.

Makes about 10 fritters

Ingredients

100g (3½oz) plain flour

50g (1¾oz) cornflour (for extra crispiness)

½ tsp sea salt

½ tsp freshly ground black pepper

½ tsp smoked paprika

½ tsp ground cumin

½ tsp baking powder

1 egg

100ml (3½fl oz) sparkling water, soda water, or pale ale (ice cold)

1 tbsp soy sauce

1 tsp lemon juice

1 small garlic clove, finely grated

200g (7oz) spring onions, finely sliced

50g (1¾oz) feta

Vegetable oil, for frying

Flaky sea salt

1. Mix the flour, cornflour, salt, pepper, smoked paprika, cumin, and baking powder. In a separate bowl, whisk the egg, sparkling water, soy sauce, and lemon juice until combined.

2. Gradually pour the wet ingredients into the dry while whisking to form a smooth batter. Stir in the garlic and spring onions then crumble in the feta and gently mix. The batter should be thick enough to coat a spoon but not overly runny.

3. Heat 2–3cm (1in) of oil in a deep pan over a medium–high heat until it reaches 180°C (350°F), or until a drop of batter sizzles and rises immediately.

4. Drop heaped tablespoons of the batter into the hot oil, frying in batches to avoid overcrowding. Cook for 2–3 minutes per side until deep golden and crisp. Lift with a slotted spoon and drain on kitchen paper.

5. Serve piping hot with a sprinkle of flaky salt and your choice of dips and sides.

Dips to pair with …

Delicious dips to serve with these fritters include:

Greek yoghurt, lemon zest, garlic, and fresh herbs.

Mayo mixed with lime juice, chilli flakes, and a dash of smoked paprika.

Soy sauce, rice vinegar, sesame oil, and a touch of honey.

Brassicas

40

Cabbage

Key growing information

- All year, depending on variety
- 1cm (½in) sowing depth
- 30–50cm (12–20in) between plants, depending on variety
- 16–20 weeks to harvest
- Full sun
- Hardy
- High water needs
- Medium fertility needs
- 5 plants per sq m
- 7.2kg (16lb) per sq m

Recommended varieties

Spring (sow in mid- to late summer) 'Wheelers Imperial', 'Durham Early'; **Summer and autumn** (sow summer cabbages late winter to early spring, autumn cabbages mid- to late spring) 'Greyhound', 'Golden Acre Primo 2'; **Winter** (sow late spring) 'Savoy Cabbage Best of All' (pictured right), 'Holland Late Winter'

Growing

Cabbages are one of the understated staple crops in a kitchen garden, offering a significant quantity of food and multiple uses in the kitchen. With so many types and varieties to choose from, such as Savoy with deep-green crinkled leaves, and 'Greyhound' with a pointy head, you can easily enjoy cabbages year-round.

Spring cabbages can be eaten in early to late spring as loose-leaf cabbages, or you can allow them to develop heads to enjoy in late spring and early summer, providing a valuable food supply at that time of year.

Cabbages and some other brassicas benefit from being started in a seed bed.

STAGE 1
Sowing in a seed bed
A seed bed lets you start many seedlings in a small space – ideal if you have limited space under cover for modules. Use a rake handle to create drills 20cm (8in) apart and around 1cm (½in) deep, **sow** seeds, cover with soil, and **water**. You will get about 5 plants from every 10cm (4in) of drill.

Sowing in modules
Under cover, **sow** 2 seeds per module cell and **thin** to the strongest seedling.

STAGE 2
When sown in a seed bed
Once plants are 15cm (6in) tall, use a fork to lift the plants with their roots attached. Gently pull

all year, and will crop for a couple of growing seasons if you remove (and eat) the flower shoots in early spring. **Water** and **mulch** thoroughly and feed monthly with a liquid feed (see p.13) during the growing season.

HARVEST

Spring cabbages can be harvested as cut-and-come-again leaves or allowed to develop heads. Cabbages are ready when their heads have firmed up. Give them a gentle squeeze and if they show little resistance you can harvest them. Using a sharp knife or secateurs, cut the whole head with 2cm (¾in) of stem. Eat or compost the larger leaves surrounding the head.

each seedling apart, and **transplant** up to the first set of leaves in their final growing position. **Water** well.

When sown in modules
When seedlings have 2 or 3 true leaves, pot them into 7cm (3in) or 9cm (3½in) pots to **grow on** under cover.

STAGE 3
When transplanted from a seed bed
Consider feeding once every 3–4 weeks with a liquid **feed** (see p.13) for a boost. Cabbage responds well to a good **mulch** of 3–5cm (1–2in) of straw or grass clippings from early summer.

When sown in modules
Once seedlings have 6 or 7 true leaves, they are ready to be planted out. **Transplant** them, and consider giving a liquid **feed** every 3 weeks and applying a 3–5cm (1–2in) **mulch**.

CONTAINER GROWING
Grow 1 cabbage per container, **transplanting** from a module (stage 3). Either let it form a head, or grow a loose-leaf type to act as a cut-and-come-again supply of cabbage greens through the season. Our favourite variety for this is Asturian tree cabbage, which has an abundance of leaves

Look out for
Two types of cabbage white caterpillars adore cabbages and other spring brassicas. Large cabbage white caterpillars have black dots down their pale yellow and green bodies, while small cabbage white caterpillars are pure green. Stake netting over the top of crops to prevent butterflies laying eggs on them, without the leaves touching the netting as the butterflies can lay eggs through it. Stay vigilant, rub off any eggs, and pick off any caterpillars.
Also look out for pigeons (p.113) and slugs (p.107).

Cooking

🥄 OKONOMIYAKI

This version comes from Osaka, where *okonomiyaki* means "cooked as you like it." It's a thick, comforting cabbage pancake, in a light batter with the essential drizzle of *okonomiyaki* sauce and Japanese mayonnaise.

In Hiroshima, instead of the cabbage and batter being mixed together, the ingredients are layered with noodles. Other regions of Japan have their own twists. You can add a spoonful or two of kimchi into the mix for a spicy, fermented version.

Serves 4

Ingredients
For the batter

140g (5oz) plain flour

¼ tsp fine sea salt

¼ tsp caster sugar

¼ tsp baking powder

150g (5½oz) *nagaimo* (Chinese yam) or *yamaimo* (mountain yam), grated, or extra cabbage

180ml (6fl oz) *dashi* (kombu and/or shiitake stock)

For the filling

About ½ head (640g/1lb 6oz) green cabbage, finely shredded

30g (1oz) pickled red ginger (*beni shōga*), drained

25g (1oz) *tenkasu* (tempura scraps, optional)

To cook and serve

Neutral oil (such as peanut, rapeseed, or sunflower), for frying

2 tbsp *okonomiyaki* sauce (or mix 1 tbsp ketchup with 1 tbsp Worcestershire sauce)

2 tbsp Japanese mayonnaise (or plant-based mayonnaise)

Aonori seaweed flakes or chopped spring onions (optional)

1. In a large bowl, whisk together the flour, salt, sugar, and baking powder. Stir in the yam and *dashi* until smooth. Rest for 30–60 minutes if possible.

2. Fold the cabbage, pickled ginger, and *tenkasu* (if using) into the batter until everything is well coated.

3. Heat a little oil in a frying pan over a medium heat. Spoon in one-quarter of the mixture, shaping into a round about 15cm (6in) wide and 3cm (1in) thick. Cover and cook for 5 minutes, until golden underneath. Flip with care and cook uncovered for another 5 minutes. Repeat with the remaining mixture.

4. Slide each pancake onto a plate. Brush with *okonomiyaki* sauce, then drizzle with mayonnaise in zigzags. Scatter with *aonori* or spring onions if you like. Serve immediately, cut into wedges like a cake or pie.

Chinese Cabbage

Key growing information

- 🌱 Early spring to midsummer
- ↓ 1cm (½in) sowing depth
- ↔ 30–35cm (12–14in) between plants
- 🗓 10–12 weeks to harvest
- ☼ Partial shade
- ❄ Half hardy
- 💧 High water needs
- 🪴 Medium fertility needs
- ☐ 8 plants per sq m
- 🧺 8kg (17½lb) per sq m

Recommended varieties

'Yuki', 'Wong Bok'

Growing

Also known as napa cabbage, this is one of the most productive crops you can grow due to its rapid growth rate. A must-try, this is a staple crop in East Asian countries, and thrives elsewhere if it has plenty of water during hot periods.

STAGE 1
Sow 2 seeds per module cell under cover and thin to the strongest.

STAGE 2
Once 3 true leaves have developed, **pot on** into 7cm (3in) pots.

STAGE 3
Plant out when 6–8 true leaves have developed. Keep well watered during their lifetime for best results.

CONTAINER GROWING
Grow 3 seedlings (stage 3) per container, spaced towards the edges so they all have space to mature.

HARVEST
Harvest when the heads are firm when squeezed. Cut at soil level, and strip and compost the outer leaves, and then the cabbages are ready for the kitchen.

Look out for
Slugs may eat the leaves of Chinese cabbage plants. They will devour smaller seedlings, so growing the seedlings to 6–8 true leaves before planting out will help minimize damage. Further measures include applying slug nematodes to your soil before sowing (once in late winter and again in mid-spring); these microscopic organisms target and kill slugs. You can also do a slug hunt in the early evening on 3 consecutive nights, repeating this hunt on a monthly basis from late spring to midsummer.

Cooking

🗋 KIMCHI

A cultural and culinary powerhouse from South Korea, this side dish preserves your winter greens for the hungry gap and adds flavour to your meals.

Makes 3.5kg (7lb)

Ingredients

2 medium Chinese (napa) cabbages

150g (5½oz) coarse sea salt (non-iodized)

For the kimchi paste

60g (2oz) glutinous rice flour

240ml (8fl oz) water

2 tbsp sugar

60ml (2fl oz) fish sauce or soy sauce (vegan)

6 garlic cloves, minced

2.5cm (1in) ginger, peeled and grated

1 small onion, diced

30g (1oz) fermented salted shrimp or miso (vegan)

Small bunch of *minari* or flat-leaf parsley, finely chopped

120g (4½oz) *gochugaru*

1 small (200g/7oz) daikon radish or carrot, julienned

4 spring onions, chopped

Equipment

2 x 2 litre (3½ pint) glass jars with lids, sterilized (see p.28), or specialized kimchi boxes from Korea

Knife

Chopping board

Large mixing bowl

Small saucepan

2 glass fermentation weights

Food-safe gloves (optional)

1. Quarter the cabbages lengthwise, keeping some of the core attached to each piece so that the leaves stay together. Place in a large bowl, salt generously, and massage the salt between the layers. Let it sit for 2–3 hours, turning occasionally, until it is softened and releasing water.

2. In a saucepan, mix the glutinous rice flour with half of the water to form a smooth paste. Stir in the remaining water, then cook over medium–high heat, stirring for 5 minutes until thickened. Add the sugar, stir to dissolve, then remove from the heat and cool.

3. Once cool, mix in the fish sauce (or soy), garlic, ginger, onion, salted shrimp (or miso), *minari* (or parsley), and *gochugaru* (for a shortcut, blend these ingredients first). Stir in the julienned radish and spring onions.

4. Rinse the cabbage thoroughly to remove excess salt, then drain well. Spread the kimchi paste between the leaves. Wear gloves to avoid stains and irritation.

5. Fold each quarter into a compact bundle and pack into a sterilized container, pressing with the glass weights to remove air pockets. Leave 3cm (1in) at the top for expansion. Seal the jar and leave to ferment at room temperature (18–21°C/65–70°F), out of direct sunlight, for 3–5 days, opening briefly each day for pressure to escape.

6. Open it and have a sniff. It should smell tangy and delicious. Taste a little. If you'd rather it be more potent, give it a few more days. Look out for surface mould on any ingredients that are dry above the brine for too long. If this happens, discard the spoiled part and weigh down ingredients below the liquid. If it smells yeasty or foul, don't eat it.

7. Once it's to your liking, seal tightly and refrigerate. The flavour peaks after 2 weeks to a month and stays delicious for 2 months before turning very sour and soft.

Tip
If this recipe looks a little daunting, stick with just the cabbage (450g) and salt (9g), shred the cabbage, and make sauerkraut instead.

Cauliflower

Key growing information

- Mid-spring to midsummer
- 1cm (½in) sowing depth
- 50cm (20in) between plants
- 14–20 weeks to harvest
- Full sun
- Hardy
- Medium water needs
- High fertility needs
- 4 plants per sq m
- 5kg (11lb) per sq m

Recommended varieties

'All the Year Round' (pictured top right), 'Autumn Giant', 'Candid Charm', 'Di Sicilia Violetto' (pictured bottom right)

Growing

Cauliflowers need a nutritionally rich soil, and respond well to liquid feeds. Sufficient fertility will yield large heads that are a delight in the kitchen.

STAGE 1

Sowing in a seed bed
See cabbage for all stages, page 104.

Sowing in modules
Sow 2 seeds per module cell under cover and keep moist. **Thin** to the strongest one.

STAGE 2

When sown in modules
Pot on seedlings into a 7cm (3in) or 9cm (3½in) pot once they have 2 or 3 true leaves.

STAGE 3

When sown in modules
Plant out when seedlings have 6–8 true leaves. Add a couple of generous handfuls of compost to the base of the hole. **Water** plants well, particularly as heads form. Consider applying a liquid feed (see p.13) every 2–3 weeks from a month after planting out.

CONTAINER GROWING

Grow 1 cauliflower per container, **transplanting** when it has about 6 true leaves (stage 3). **Feed** every 2 weeks (see p.13). **Mulch** (see p.11) to retain moisture for cauliflower development.

HARVEST

Harvest when the heads are firm, white, and tightly packed. Cut around 7cm (3in) below the head to remove it from the plant. If you miss their prime they may not look as good but are still fully edible. The upper stem and leaves are edible.

Tip

For a beautiful, white head, bend one of the large leaves inwards to cover over and blanch the head when it begins developing.

Look out for

Cabbage white caterpillars (see p.105) and pigeons (see p.113) may damage plants.

Cooking

CAULIFLOWER GRATIN

This dish is a hybrid between a luxurious cauliflower cheese and a crispy, golden gratin. Serve with grilled, steamed, or roasted greens, sauerkraut, kimchi, or a zesty walnut and cabbage salad.

Serves 2

Ingredients

1 cauliflower, broken into florets

1 onion (not a red onion), finely chopped

1 garlic clove, finely chopped

4 tbsp butter

Sea salt

Freshly ground black pepper

35g (1oz) plain flour

70ml (2½fl oz) double cream

Fresh oregano, sage, or thyme

180g (6oz) grated cheese (Emmental, Gruyère, or Cheddar)

Pinch of nutmeg

100g (3½oz) breadcrumbs

¼ tsp garlic granules

1. Preheat the oven to 190°C (170°C fan/375°F/Gas 5). Blanch the cauliflower florets in salted boiling water for 3–4 minutes. Reserve the leaves for a side salad.

2. Sauté the onion and garlic in butter, with a pinch of salt and pepper, in a deep ovenproof pan until soft and sweet.

3. Add the flour to the onion mixture and stir to make a roux, then add the cream, herbs, cheese, and nutmeg and continue to stir until the sauce is thick and smooth.

4. Drain the cauliflower and mix the florets into the sauce, then top with breadcrumbs and a pinch of garlic granules.

5. Bake for 30 minutes until golden and crispy.

Meal prep
Freeze portions before adding the breadcrumbs. Thaw in a fridge overnight, top with breadcrumbs, then bake for 30 minutes at the temperature given above.

Brassicas

Broccoli

Key growing information

- Early spring to early summer
- 1cm (½in) sowing depth
- 35–40cm (14–16in) between plants
- 16–40 weeks to harvest, depending on variety
- Full sun
- Hardy
- Medium water needs
- High fertility needs
- 4 plants per sq m
- 1.6–1.8kg (3½–4lb) per sq m

Recommended varieties

Calabrese (ready in 16 weeks) 'Belstar', 'Fiesta';
Sprouting (ready in 40 weeks) 'Claret' (purple, pictured far right), 'Burbank' (white)

Growing

There are two types of broccoli: calabrese (heads, pictured above) and sprouting (flower stems, pictured above right). Calabrese is typically sown and harvested in the same growing season, while sprouting is ready to harvest in late winter to early spring the following year, though this will vary between varieties.

STAGE 1
Sowing in a seed bed
See cabbage for all stages, page 104.

Sowing in modules
Sow 2 seeds per module under cover, keeping them well watered. **Thin** to the strongest plant if both seeds germinate.

STAGE 2
When sown in modules
Once the seedlings have 4 or 5 leaves, **pot on** into 7cm (3in) or 9cm (3½in) pots under cover, burying the stem of the seedling up to the first leaf.

STAGE 3
When sown in modules
Once seedlings are 15–20cm (6–8in) in height, they are ready to **plant out**. Add a generous handful of compost to the planting hole, and you can plant the seedling either at the same depth as it was growing in the pot, or up to the first set of leaves if the stem has continued to lengthen.

HARVEST
Calabrese
Calabrese is ready to harvest when the head is 10–15cm (4–6in) across. To harvest, cut the stem around 10cm (4in) below the main head. The plant may create some

additional smaller heads if you leave it in the ground. The leaves are also edible, but the stem of the head is a delicacy! Simply peel the outer layer, slice into 1cm (1/2in) slices, and pan fry.

Sprouting
Sprouting broccoli will usually create one main central head with multiple side shoots. Harvest by cutting or snapping off the shoots (pictured above) at a length of 10–15cm (4–6in).

Tip
You only have around a week to harvest broccoli in its prime before the flower shoots begin to "blow". This is when the flowers begin to emerge. If you're a little late to harvest, don't worry, it's still edible and can be cooked in the same way.

Look out for
In some areas, pigeons enjoy feasting on brassicas, including broccoli. This can devastate crops. The best way to avoid this damage is to net your plants should this happen. They may already be netted if you want to prevent cabbage white caterpillars (see p.105). Look out also for wind damage (see p.118).

Cooking

Most recipes work well with any type of broccoli you have and you can use stems, leaves, and florets.

🔪 BROCCOLI AND SHEEP'S CURD TART

This is a proper tart – one of those solid, satisfying centrepieces that makes lunch feel like a feast and dinner like a treat. This buttery, rustic shortcrust pastry is filled with tender broccoli florets and tangy sheep's curd – the fresh, slightly grassy cousin of feta. Both types of broccoli work here, but calabrese will need chopping up more. Serve with a pot of chutney and a handful of fresh salad.

Serves 3–4

Ingredients
For the shortcrust pastry
250g (9oz) plain flour

125g (4½oz) cold unsalted butter, cubed

Pinch of sea salt

1 egg yolk (add the white to the eggs in the filling)

For the filling
About 200g/7oz of broccoli, cut into bite-sized florets

1 leek, thinly sliced

A little olive oil or butter

3 large eggs

200ml (7fl oz) double cream

1 tbsp Dijon mustard

Sea salt

Freshly ground black pepper

Pinch of nutmeg (optional)

150g (5½oz) sheep's curd, or ricotta or cottage cheese

1. Starting with the pastry, rub the flour and butter together with your fingertips until the mix resembles breadcrumbs. Alternatively, pulse them briefly in a food processor (if you let it run too long it will warm the butter). Stir in the salt, then the egg yolk and just enough cold water (1–2 tbsp) to bring it together into a dough. Don't overwork it as this will make the pastry tough after baking. Cover with baking parchment and chill for 30 minutes.

Broccoli

2. Meanwhile, steam or blanch the broccoli and leek for 2–3 minutes in salted water – they should still have a bit of bite. Drain and set aside to cool.

3. Preheat the oven to 200°C (180°C fan/400°F/Gas 6). Roll out the pastry on a lightly floured surface to fit a 23cm (9in) tart tin. Grease the tin with a small amount of olive oil or butter and line with the pastry. Prick the base with a fork, and chill again for 15 minutes.

4. Line the raw pastry with baking parchment and weigh it down with baking beans, then blind bake the pastry for 15 minutes. The beans hold the pastry in place while the butter melts during the initial baking. Remove the parchment and beans and bake uncovered for another 5 minutes until pale golden.

5. Whisk together the eggs, cream, mustard, and a generous pinch of salt and pepper. Add nutmeg if using.

6. Arrange the broccoli and leek in the pastry case. Dot over spoonfuls of sheep's curd. Pour over the cream and egg mixture and bake for 25–30 minutes until golden and just set, with a slight wobble. Eat warm, with peppery leaves.

Brussels Sprouts

Key growing information

- 🌱 Early spring to early summer
- ↕ 1cm (½in) sowing depth
- ↔ 40cm (16in) between plants
- 📅 16–24 weeks to harvest
- ☀ Full sun
- ❄ Hardy
- 💧 Medium water needs
- 🍃 High fertility needs
- ▢ 5 plants per sq m
- 🧺 5kg (11lb) per sq m

Recommended varieties

'Groninger' (pictured right), 'Long Island', 'Igor'

Growing

Sprouts are an undeservedly hated vegetable. However, as with anything that is homegrown, they taste so much better from the garden, plus they are a valuable winter crop.

STAGE 1
Sowing in a seed bed
See cabbage for all stages, page 104.

Sowing in modules
Under cover, **sow** 2 seeds per module cell. Keep watered and then **thin** to the strongest seedling.

STAGE 2
When sown in modules
Once the seedlings have 3 or 4 true leaves, **pot on** into 7cm (3in) or 9cm (3½in) pots to continue growing.

STAGE 3
When sown in modules
Plant out your seedlings when they are 20cm (8in) tall. Make a hole deep enough so that the first set of leaves will be at soil level, then add a handful of compost to the base of the hole. This deeper planting will encourage a stronger stem to prevent the laden plants toppling in winter. For advice on staking, if needed, see tip, p.118.

CONTAINER GROWING
Due to the shape of these plants, it is best to grow one Brussels sprout seedling per container, planting other crops around the base, such as chard, nasturtiums, or even peas, earlier in the growing season. Transplant the seedling at stage 3.

HARVEST
Harvest sprouts when they are firm in texture, either by picking off what you need from the stem, or cutting the entire stem at ground level

Cooking

🔪 SAUTÉED SPROUTS WITH CHESTNUTS

This is winter on a plate – Brussels sprouts and nutty sweetness, crisped and golden. It makes a proper side dish or a light lunch with toast and pickles, proving that sprouts don't have to be boiled into submission. Here they're halved and sautéed until just tender, with deep caramel edges, and the addition of buttery chestnuts. You can add pancetta if you like, but honestly, they don't need it. Homemade kimchi added at the end makes a delicious, spicy version.

Serves 2

Ingredients

1 tbsp butter

1 tbsp olive oil

300g (10oz) Brussels sprouts, trimmed and halved

1 garlic clove, finely sliced

180g (6oz) chestnuts, cooked and roughly broken

Sea salt

Freshly ground black pepper

A squeeze of lemon juice

1. Heat the butter and oil in a wide frying pan over a medium heat. Add the sprouts, cut-side down, and let them take on colour without moving them about too much, probably for about 5–7 minutes.

2. Once the sprouts are golden, toss in the garlic and chestnuts. Cook for a few more minutes until everything's catching and toasty. Season well with salt and black pepper, then finish with a squeeze of lemon. Serve immediately.

and stripping the sprouts. If you've missed them in their prime you have a second chance – allow the sprouts to sprout, and enjoy these tasty flower stems as you would sprouting broccoli. Sprout tops are also edible.

Look out for
Wind (see p.118) and pigeons (see p.113) may affect Brussels sprouts.

Kale

Key growing information

- Early spring to midsummer
- 1–2cm (½–¾in) sowing depth
- 30–40cm (12–16in) between plants
- 10–12 weeks to harvest
- Full sun and partial shade
- Hardy
- Medium water needs
- Medium fertility needs
- 5 plants per sq m
- 6kg (13lb) per sq m, including flower shoots

Recommended varieties

Annual 'Dwarf Green Curled' (pictured right), 'Cavolo Nero' (pictured on opposite page), 'Red Russian'; **Perennial** 'Keeper', Taunton Deane'

Growing

Kale is a hardy winter staple, offering multiple colours and textures of leaves to enjoy not only in the kitchen but also visually in the garden – you often see kale in ornamental borders due to its structure.

STAGE 1
Sowing in a seed bed
See cabbage for all stages, page 104.

Sowing in modules
Under cover, **sow** 2 seeds per module cell, and keep well watered. **Thin** to the strongest seedling.

STAGE 2
When sown in modules
Once seedlings have 3 or 4 true leaves, **pot on** into 7cm (3in) or 9cm (3½in) pots to grow on under cover until they reach around 20cm (8in) tall. Allowing them to grow to this height will not only make them more resilient to slug (see p.107) and flea beetle damage (see p.52), but will allow you to plant more deeply at stage 3.

STAGE 3
When sown in modules
When you **plant out** your kale, add a handful of additional compost at the base of the hole before burying the stem up to the first set of leaves for a more stable plant. This will make kale more resilient during dry weather, too, as the roots will be deeper, therefore more likely to access moisture further down in the soil.

Tip
If you have an exposed garden, it is a good idea to stake your kale plants in mid-autumn in preparation for storms. Find a stake around 1m (3ft) long, hammer at least 30cm (12in) of it into the ground, and tie the stem to the stake in at least two places.

Kale

CONTAINER GROWING

Plant 1 kale plant (stage 3) in a container for large leaves and flower shoots the following spring, or 3 kale plants as a productive leaf crop during the growing season. If you grow 3, select 1 to remain over the winter, cutting off the other two at the base. If you opt for just 1 plant, consider planting a couple of annual flowers, like nasturtium (see p.202) or calendula (see p.206), for colour and to fill the space. A crop of direct-sown radish (see p.50) would also work.

HARVEST

Pick a few leaves from each plant by gently pulling down and away, focusing on the lower leaves. As the weeks progress you will notice that the stem of the kale gets longer in response to the harvesting. Avoid taking more than one-third of the leaves at any one time.

At the end of winter, allow your kale to create flower stems to harvest in the same way you would for sprouting broccoli (see p.113) as an additional harvest. Consider leaving a couple of kale plants to flower as they are a much-needed early spring nectar source for pollinators.

Tip

If you are a kale lover, consider growing a perennial kale plant, such as 'Keeper' or 'Taunton Deane', which will live for around 5 years, giving you leafy harvests all year. You can then create more perennial kale plants by taking cuttings 20cm (8in) long from the stem, removing all but the top two leaves. This is best done between midwinter and mid-spring, but can work year-round. Bury each cutting to three-quarters of its depth in a pot and plant out after about 6 weeks, once it has rooted well.

Look out for

Cabbage white caterpillars (see p.105), slugs (see p.107), and pigeons (see p.113) may damage kale.

Cooking

KALE SMOOTHIE

I've heard a lot of nonsense spoken about green smoothies, as though they're punishment rather than pleasure. But a good one, made with fresh garden ingredients and a bit of know-how, is earthy, vibrant, and properly delicious.

This one's based around that dependable winter workhorse, kale, but the bones of the recipe are loose. Swap things in, switch things out – the method's the same, allowing you to make a thick, refreshing meal-in-a-glass from all of your homegrown goodies. It's great for using up a glut, too. Drink it outside, if you can. It tastes better that way.

Serves 1

Ingredients
1 large handful of kale leaves, stripped from the stalks

1 apple or pear, cored and chopped (no need to peel)

1/2 banana (frozen is ideal, for texture)

Juice of 1/2 lemon

A thumb-sized piece of fresh ginger

250ml (9fl oz) cold water or oat milk

1 tbsp nut butter and/or 1 tbsp flax seeds and/or a spoon of yoghurt (optional)

1. Pop everything into a blender. Whizz until smooth, stopping to scrape down the sides if needed.

2. Try the smoothie for taste and texture – it should be bright, creamy, and not too thick. Add more liquid if it's closer to a purée, then pour into a glass.

Alternative recipe
If you make a thick smoothie or you're dealing with a glut and make far too much, you can turn it into a granita. Freeze it in a plastic storage container, opening it every hour or so to scrape with a fork. After two or three goes, the granita should be light and fluffy ice crystals, perfect to enjoy as a bowl of something cold and refreshing on a hot day in the garden.

Twists to try …

Fresh ingredients you can add to your smoothie include carrots, beetroot, strawberries, pears – you name it. There are also less common ingredients, such as rose or cornflower petals, blackcurrant leaf, or lemon verbena. It's easy to get creative and quickly make something you'd never find in a supermarket. Here are more suggestions:

Leafy greens Swap kale for spinach, chard, or beet leaves. For older leaves, blanch first. They may need a little help to be tasty, so add some ginger root.

Fruit Use apples and pears as great bases, crisp and slightly sweet.

Roots Peel and grate carrots and beetroot then steam and cool before adding to give sweetness and body.

Extras Add a spoonful of kefir or yoghurt for tang and goodness. A dash of apple cider vinegar gives a kick.

Herbs Lift the whole thing with a few mint or parsley leaves. Coriander works well with carrot and apple. Lemon verbena and rose offer a sophisticated twist.

Kale

Pak Choi

Key growing information

- 🌱 Early spring to midsummer
- ↕ 1cm (½in) sowing depth
- ↔ 25cm (10in) between plants
- 📅 6–8 weeks to harvest
- ☀ Full sun and partial shade
- ❄ Half hardy
- 💧 High water needs
- 🌿 Medium fertility needs
- ▢ 15 plants per sq m
- 🧺 4.2kg (9¼lb) per sq m

Recommended varieties

'Joi Choi' (pictured right), 'Red Choi'

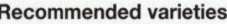

Growing

STAGE 1
Sow 2 seeds per module under cover, keep them watered, and **thin** to the strongest seedling.

STAGE 2
Once 4 or 5 true leaves have developed, **plant out** into their final growing position.

STAGE 3
Water regularly in dry spells.

CONTAINER GROWING
Plant out 4 seedlings (stage 2) at equal spacings.

HARVEST
Gently twist the whole plant from the soil, then cut off the roots with a sharp knife.

Cooking

PAK CHOI IN THE KITCHEN
Pak choi brings a gentle crunch and subtle mustardy sweetness. Its juicy white stems and tender green leaves hold up well to heat, yet are delicate enough to eat raw. The stems take a minute or so longer to cook than the leaves.

Stir it through noodle soups at the last minute, toss it into stir-fries, or char it in a hot pan with sesame oil for smoky depth. It pairs well with soy, miso, ginger, garlic, and chilli, as well as creamy ingredients like tahini, goat's cheese, or peanut butter. For contrast, try serving pak choi with sharp citrus, pickled vegetables, or vinegar. Stir it into curries just before serving, or blend it into pestos and pasta sauces.

Use the crisp stems in noodle salads. Slice it raw into fine ribbons and toss it through slaws (see opposite) with sesame dressing. Or ferment it into a quick sauerkraut or kimchi (see p.108).

Kohl Rabi

Key growing information

- Early spring to midsummer
- 1cm (½in) sowing depth
- 15–20cm (6–8in) between plants
- 8–12 weeks to harvest
- Full sun
- Half hardy
- Medium water needs
- Medium fertility needs
- 20 plants per sq m
- 4.5kg (10lb) per sq m

Recommended varieties

'Purple Delicacy' (pictured right), 'Delicacy White', 'Superschmelz'

Growing

STAGE 1
Sow 1 seed per module cell under cover and **water** well.

STAGE 2
Once seedlings have 3 or 4 true leaves, **plant out** into holes 15–20cm (6–8in) apart.

STAGE 3
Water well in dry spells to encourage the stem to swell.

CONTAINER GROWING
Plant out 5 kohl rabi (stage 2) at equal spacings.

HARVEST
Harvest the swollen stems from 5cm (2in) in diameter by cutting at the base of the plant. Leaves are edible.

Cooking

KOHL RABI SLAW

Mild, sweet, and crunchy, this is perfect grated into a spicy coleslaw. Get creative with veg such as carrot, cabbage, spring onions, or beetroot, and herbs like chives, sage, and oregano.

Makes 4 or 5 large portions

2 kohl rabi, grated

1 apple, julienned

1 unwaxed lemon, zest and juice

¼ of a cabbage, shredded

A handful of chives or sage

2 tbsp mayonnaise

1 tbsp wholegrain mustard

¼ tsp wasabi

A pinch of garlic granules

Sea salt and freshly ground black pepper to taste

1. Prepare and mix all the ingredients together and serve at once.

Legumes

LO
O

Peas

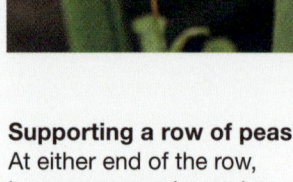

Key growing information

- 🫴 Early spring to early summer
- ❄ Hardy
- ↕ 2cm (³/₄in) sowing depth
- 💧 Medium water needs
- ↔ 10cm (4in) between clumps
- 🕯 Medium fertility needs
- 📅 14 weeks to harvest
- ▢ 350 plants per sq m
- ☀ Full sun
- 🪣 6kg (13lb) per sq m

Recommended varieties

Garden peas 'Ambassador' (pictured far right), 'Hurst Greenshaft' (pictured right); **Mangetout** 'Oregon Sugar Pod'; **Sugarsnap** 'Nairobi'.

Growing

There are three main types of pea. Garden peas are the ones you pod. Sugarsnap and mangetout are the ones where you eat pod and pea in one, though sugarsnap have rounder pods, while mangetout (pictured above) have crunchy, flatter pods.

STAGE 1
In modules under cover, **sow** 3 or 4 seeds per cell. Don't let the compost dry out, but avoid watering too much.

STAGE 2
Pea plants need support to prevent them growing along the ground as this can cause pest and disease issues. Decide on the planting layout so you can **prepare the supports**. You can plant them in rows with either 1 or 2 lines of peas: for 2 lines, stagger the planting. Alternatively plant as a block such as a square metre with even spacing between all the plants. The support will vary according to how you decide to plant.

Check your seed packets for the height of your variety, and choose stakes that are about 30cm (1ft) taller than the mature height.

Supporting a row of peas
At either end of the row, hammer a wooden stake at least 30cm (1ft) into the ground. Place either chicken wire or netting between the 2 stakes for the peas to climb up, or string garden twine between the stakes to create a "fence" for the same purpose.

Supporting a block of peas
Create a "boxing ring" support structure by placing canes or stakes around the perimeter and stringing twine between them to create a fence. Then crisscross the

twine to the different edges to create a web to support the peas as they grow.

STAGE 3
Once seedlings are 7cm (3in) tall they are ready to **plant out** next to their supports. Plant as a clump, with all the seedlings from a module cell together. Use a trowel to create holes the size of the rootball and press the seedling roots firmly into the ground. **Water** well.

CONTAINER GROWING
Fill a container with clumps of seedlings spaced 10cm (4in) apart. To support the plants, push canes a little longer than the height of the variety into the pot, and make a web of string similar to supporting a block of peas.

HARVEST
Harvest both garden and sugarsnap peas if the pods are firm when gently squeezed. If you are after the peas, take the "stem" of the pod and pull down like a zip. This makes it easier to open the pod along this seam and reveal the peas. Mangetout are ready when pods have started to swell. Pea shoots and flowers are also edible.

Look out for
Pigeons may eat the shoots and strip the leaves. To prevent this, choose shorter varieties of peas (around 60cm/2ft) and create a growing cage or dome with chicken wire that will remain over and above the mature peas. This is plastic-free and doesn't visually stand out like netting does; painting the chicken wire with black paint will make it even less conspicuous. Rodents can also damage pea plants (see p.134).

Cooking

GARDEN PEA AND KOREAN MINT RISOTTO

There's something lovely about making risotto with what's growing just outside your door. A bit of stirring, a bit of steam on the windows, and a bowl of something creamy and green by the end of it. This version celebrates peas and Korean mint (see p.161), with its softly herbal, almost aniseed brightness. Together, they make a risotto that's light but satisfying, and surprisingly elegant for its simplicity. If you don't have Korean mint, tarragon or basil would also work well.

Serves 2

Ingredients

1 tbsp butter, plus extra to finish

3 tbsp olive oil

1 small onion, finely chopped

Sea salt

1 garlic clove, minced

200g (7oz) risotto rice (Arborio)

150ml (5fl oz) dry white wine (or 50ml/1¾fl oz apple cider vinegar)

800ml (1½ pints) hot vegetable stock

300g (10oz) garden peas (fresh or frozen; see tip)

A small handful of Korean mint leaves, finely chopped, plus extra to top

30g (1oz) hard cheese (Parmesan or a vegetarian equivalent), grated

Freshly ground black pepper, to taste

1. Heat the butter and oil in a wide pan. Gently cook the onion with a pinch of salt for 15 minutes or so until soft. Add the garlic and cook for a minute more.

2. Tip in the rice and stir to coat each grain in the buttery mix. After a minute or two the grains will start to look translucent. Pour in the wine (or apple cider vinegar) and let it bubble away until absorbed.

3. Now the relaxing bit. Add a ladleful of the hot stock and simmer until all liquid has been absorbed by the rice, stirring often. Then add another ladleful, and continue for 20–25 minutes, until the rice is creamy but still has a bit of bite.

4. Stir in the peas for the last 3–4 minutes of cooking – they should stay bright and just tender. Off the heat, fold in the Korean mint, cheese, and another knob of butter. Season well with salt and pepper. Serve warm, with a few torn mint leaves on top.

Tip
To save on time, you can use sugarsnap peas instead of garden peas (or a mix of the two), and skip the need to pod them. If you're using older peas, add them a little earlier and let them cook through.

Alternative recipe
Try swapping out the rice for barley. Soak the barley in water with a pinch of salt and a spoonful of yoghurt for 12–24 hours before cooking to speed up cooking time and give the barley a tangy, chewy bounce.

Climbing Beans

Key growing information

- Mid-spring to early summer
- 2–3cm (1in) sowing depth
- 20–30cm (8–12in)
- 14 weeks to harvest
- Full sun
- Tender
- High water needs
- Medium fertility needs
- 10 plants per sq m
- 6kg (13lb) per sq m

Recommended varieties

Runner beans 'Scarlet Emperor' (pictured right and far right), 'Czar'; **French beans** 'Cobra', 'Blue Lake'.

Growing

Climbing beans are easy to grow and very productive. Some have stunning flowers as an added benefit, and their height adds structure to the garden. There are two main types of climbing beans: French beans have thin, rounded tender pods, while runner beans produce large, flat pods.

STAGE 1

Sow 1 seed per deep module cell (see p.8) or toilet roll tube filled with compost. Keep in a warm, bright area under cover, protected from frosts to aid germination.

STAGE 2

Create your **support** structure before you plant out the beans. Each cane should be around 2.5m (8ft) long, and will support 1 plant. Push 10–12 canes into the ground at equal spacings to form a circle around 80cm (32in) in diameter. Tie at the top with twine, bending the canes in to create a cone structure.

STAGE 3

When seedlings are 15cm (6in) tall they are ready to **transplant**. Around 5cm (2in) away from the outside or inside of each support cane, push your trowel deep into the ground and angle it away from the cane to create a pocket. Plant the seedling into this pocket, lift the trowel up and out, and then firm in the soil around the roots. **Water** thoroughly.

Tip
As the plants grow, ensure the leading shoot grows up its designated cane. If it is growing off elsewhere, help it back onto the right cane by gently wrapping the shoot clockwise up and around it.

CONTAINER GROWING

Push four 2.5m (8ft) canes down to the base of the container around the edge and tie them together at the top to create a cone shape. On the inside of each cane, **plant** 1 seedling (using the same technique as at stage 3), and water in. Keep well watered, particularly during flowering, as this helps with pollination for pod formation.

HARVEST

For tender runner beans, harvest the pods when they are 15–20cm (6–8in) long. Pick French beans at 10–15cm (4–6in) long. Carefully pinch the pods away from the plant to prevent ripping off large sections. Mature beans can be harvested at the end of the season (pictured right), dried, and used in soups and stews. Runner bean flowers are also edible.

Look out for
Slugs often target younger climbing bean seedlings (see p.107).

Cooking

CHARRED RUNNER BEANS AND TROUT

This is a dish that tastes like late summer: fat runner beans, still squeaky and green, charred at the edges; a fillet of rainbow trout, richer than salmon, but gentle and buttery, crisp-skinned, and soft in the middle. And then preserved lemon: salty, sharp, and deeply fragrant, with just a hint of bitterness to balance the dish. It's simple food, but the kind that makes you stop and notice every mouthful.

The beans do most of the talking here, with their smoky sweetness and soft bite. The trout is cooked hot and fast, and the lemon lifts it all into something fresh. This is garden and river in a single dish – green, clean, and packed with flavour. Serve with a crisp glass of white, some new potatoes, and maybe a blob of aïoli on the side.

Serves 2

Ingredients

200g (7oz) runner beans, topped and tailed

1 tbsp olive oil, plus extra for cooking

Sea salt

Freshly ground black pepper

2 fillets of line-caught rainbow trout, skin on

1 tsp butter

½ preserved lemon, finely chopped (discard any inner flesh)

A few sprigs of dill or parsley, chopped

Lemon juice (optional)

1. Slice the runner beans on the diagonal. Toss them in a little olive oil with a pinch of salt. Heat a dry griddle or heavy frying pan until it's very hot, then char the beans in batches, a minute or two each side until blackened in spots and tender-crisp. Set aside.

2. Season the trout fillets with salt and pepper. Heat a little oil and butter in a pan over a medium–high heat and place the trout skin-side down, pressing gently with a spatula to keep the skin flat. Cook for 4 minutes until the skin is crisp and the flesh is mostly opaque. Flip and cook for 30 seconds to a minute more.

3. Move the trout to one side of the pan and briefly toss in the charred beans, preserved lemon, and herbs to warm and coat them. Taste and add a squeeze of fresh lemon if it needs a bit of acidity.

4. Serve at once, piling the beans onto warm plates and topping with the trout, skin-side up. Spoon over any pan juices.

Dwarf Beans

Key growing information

- Mid-spring to midsummer
- 2–3cm (1in) sowing depth
- 20cm (8in) between plants
- 12 weeks to harvest
- Full sun
- Tender
- Medium water needs
- Medium fertility needs
- 25 plants per sq m
- 5kg (11lb) per sq m

Recommended varieties

'Annabel' (pictured right), 'Amethyst', 'Safari'

Growing

Small but mighty, dwarf beans (also known as bush beans) are a great way to grow food where little gaps appear in the garden – helped particularly by their long sowing period.

STAGE 1
Sow 1 seed per cell in module trays under cover. Keep moist but do not overwater as the seeds can easily rot if too wet.

STAGE 2
Plant out when seedlings are at least 10cm (4in) in height and the risk of frost has passed. Make a hole the size of the rootball, press the rootball firmly into the hole, and **water** in.

STAGE 3
Plants may need propping up with twigs to **support** them as they tend to flop under the weight of the developing beans.

CONTAINER GROWING
Plant 4 or 5 plants per container at equal spacings.

HARVEST
Harvest when the pods are about 10cm (4in) in length or longer. Gently pull them away from the plant with one hand, holding the plant with the other so you don't accidentally rip the whole plant out of the ground.

Look out for
Rodents such as voles and mice can dig up seeds after sowing or nip young seedlings. This can be avoided by placing pots and module trays on a hanging wire shelf in a polytunnel out of reach, or by growing inside on a bright sunny windowsill until seedlings are 5cm (2in) tall. Slugs can also be a problem (see p.107).

Cooking

🔪 TEMPURA DWARF BEANS

These crisp little snacks are dangerously moreish. Dwarf beans are tender, slender, and just the right size for dipping. Cloaked in a light, lacy batter and fried until golden, they are crunchy outside, sweet and juicy within. Served as a side or a snack with drinks, they vanish faster than you'd think, so make plenty.

Serves 2

Ingredients

Oil, for deep frying (cold-pressed sunflower or rapeseed)

100g (3½oz) plain flour

1 tbsp cornflour

Pinch of fine sea salt

150ml (5fl oz) ice-cold sparkling water

150g (5½oz) dwarf beans, topped (no need to tail)

1. Heat your oil to 180°C (350°F) in a small saucepan (half-filled will do).

2. To make the batter, mix the flour, cornflour, and a pinch of salt in a bowl. Add the cold sparkling water and stir very lightly. Avoid overmixing – lumps are fine as long as the flour is wet.

3. Working in small batches, dip the beans into the batter and place them straight into the hot oil, but don't overcrowd the pan. Fry for 2–3 minutes, turning if needed, until puffed and golden.

4. Drain on kitchen paper and sprinkle with salt immediately. They are best served hot, with a wedge of lemon or a little dipping sauce, soy, ponzu, whipped feta, hummus, or something with garlic and vinegar.

Tip
Looking for a naughty twist? Try ice-cold lager instead of cold, sparkling water.

Alternative recipe
Mix it up by adding ground cumin and curry powder to the batter and serving with mango chutney and a handful of fresh coriander.

Fava Beans

Key growing information

- Late winter to late spring
- 5cm (2in) sowing depth
- 20cm (8in) between plants
- 14 weeks to harvest
- Full sun
- Hardy
- Medium water needs
- Medium fertility needs
- 25 plants per sq m
- 5kg (11lb) per sq m

Recommended varieties

Broad beans 'Ratio', 'Aquadulce Claudia', 'Crimson flowered'; **Field beans** 'Vespa' (pictured right)

Growing

Fava beans come in two main types: broad beans and smaller field beans. Both have a similar yield, are easy to grow, and are abundant. Field beans are often used for green manure but are also delicious to eat. Which to grow is down to you: broad beans have large beans but fewer pods, while field beans have smaller beans but more pods. We've found field beans work better in poorer-quality soil.

STAGE 1

Using deep module cells (see p.8) or toilet rolls under cover, fill with compost and **plant** 1 seed in each.

STAGE 2

Transplant seedlings at 10–15cm (4–6in) tall. Push your trowel vertically into the ground, angling it away from you to create a pocket in which to place the rootball. Pull the trowel out and press around the plant base.

STAGE 3

Mulch plants with grass clippings when they are around 30cm (12in) tall to help retain moisture, which will aid the bean formation. They rarely need support.

CONTAINER GROWING

Plant 3 seedlings (stage 2) per container spaced equally.

HARVEST

Harvest when the pods are firm when squeezed. Prise each pod apart with your fingers to remove the beans. Harvest the bean "tops", 7–10 edible leaves above the flowers (see below).

Look out for

Blackfly are black aphids that suck the sap from plants, impacting vigour and yield. They enjoy tender growth, which is why they target the tips of plants. Prevent blackfly issues by harvesting bean "tops" when the plants begin flowering. Fava beans are favourites of voles and mice (see p.134).

Cooking

🥄 BROAD BEAN FALAFEL

In this soft, crispy alternative to chickpea falafel, the broad beans offer a vibrant sweetness. It's delicious cold in lunchboxes the next day.

Serves 4 (makes around 16 falafel balls)

Ingredients

400g (14oz) podded broad beans (1kg/2¼lb in pods)

½ small onion or 2 spring onions, finely chopped

2 garlic cloves

A handful of fresh parsley

A handful of fresh coriander or mint

1 tsp ground cumin

1 tsp ground coriander

Sea salt and freshly ground black pepper

½ tsp baking powder

3 tbsp gram flour (or plain flour)

Oil for frying

Grated courgette or wild garlic in season (optional)

1. Blanch the broad beans for 1–2 minutes, then cool and double pod (pop them from their grey skins).

2. In a food processor, crush the beans with the onion, garlic, herbs, spices, and seasoning until coarse. Add baking powder and gram flour to bind, then chill the mixture for 20 minutes.

3. Form into walnut-sized balls. Heat about 1cm (½in) of oil in a deep pan or frying pan, and fry in batches for about 5 minutes per side until golden and crisp. Drain on kitchen paper before cooling so they don't turn greasy. Add a little more flour to the mix if the falafels break apart when frying.

4. Serve warm in flatbreads with cucumber yoghurt, salad leaves, or fermented veg.

Leafy Greens

60

Chard

Key growing information

- Early spring to midsummer
- 1cm (1/2in) sowing depth
- 25cm (10in) between plants
- 10 weeks to harvest
- Full sun and partial shade
- Hardy
- High water needs
- Medium fertility needs
- 16 plants per sq m
- 8kg (17 1/2lb) per sq m

Recommended varieties

'Rainbow Mix', 'Peppermint' (pictured right), 'Fordhook Giant', 'Perpetual Spinach'

Growing

A resilient and vigorous crop, chard provides a continuous harvesting period over many months for very little effort.

STAGE 1
Sow 1 seed per module under cover. Chard seeds are often clusters that contain 2–5 actual seeds. **Thin** to the strongest seedling once germinated.

STAGE 2
Plant out chard when seedlings have 4 or 5 true leaves. Make a hole slightly deeper than the rootball, plant the seedling, firm around the roots, and **water** well.

STAGE 3
Around 4–6 weeks after planting out, consider **mulching** your chard plants with grass clippings. Consistent moisture helps to prevent bolting (see p.142).

CONTAINER GROWING
Plant module-grown seedlings 20cm (8in) apart when growing in containers. **Water** regularly and **mulch** them with grass clippings to maintain soil moisture.

HARVEST
Pick the larger stems first by gently pulling away and down to snap them from the base of the plant. Take 2 or 3 stems at a time per plant and allow the smaller stems to continue growing.

Tip
If you're just after the baby leaves, sow chard as for lettuce (see p.142), but thin to 1 plant every 5cm (2in).

Look out for
If you see strange brown patches or squiggles on your chard leaves this will be leaf miners – tiny insects that burrow in leaves, eating the plant tissue. While they won't kill your plants, they do lower harvest quality, so remove and compost any affected leaves.

Cooking

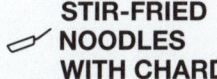
STIR-FRIED NOODLES WITH CHARD

This savoury, slurpy noodle dish includes vibrantly green and delicious chard, earthy mushrooms, and a glossy, flavoursome sauce that's both comforting and quick to cook.

Serves 2

Ingredients

150g (5½oz) dried wheat noodles or rice noodles

1 tbsp neutral oil (such as sunflower or groundnut)

2 garlic cloves, finely chopped

1 thumb-sized piece of ginger, grated

200g (7oz) mushrooms (shiitake, chestnut, or mixed), sliced

Sea salt

100g (3½oz) chard, stems and leaves separated, chopped

1 tbsp soy sauce

1 tbsp dark soy sauce (or extra regular soy)

1 tsp toasted sesame oil

1 tsp rice vinegar or lime juice

½ tsp honey

Toasted sesame seeds or chopped peanuts, to garnish

2 spring onions, finely sliced

Chilli flakes or fresh sliced chilli (optional)

1. Cook the noodles according to the packet instructions, then drain, rinse with cold water, and toss with a little oil to prevent sticking.

2. Heat a wok or large frying pan over medium–high heat. Add the oil, and fry the garlic and ginger for 30 seconds until fragrant, then add the mushrooms and a pinch of salt. Cook for 5–10 minutes, stirring occasionally, until the mushrooms are golden and tender.

3. Add the chard stems first and cook for 1–2 minutes, then add the leaves and stir until wilted.

4. Stir in the soy sauce, dark soy, sesame oil, rice vinegar (or lime juice), and honey. Add the noodles and toss everything together over a high heat for a minute or two until the mixture is glossy and hot all the way through.

5. Taste and adjust with more soy or vinegar if needed. Serve sprinkled with sesame seeds or nuts, spring onions, and chilli if you like heat.

Lettuce

Key growing information

- Mid-spring to late summer
- 1cm (½in) sowing depth
- 10cm (4in) between plants
- 8 weeks to harvest
- Full sun (spring and autumn), or partial shade (summer)
- Half hardy (will survive light frost)
- High water needs
- Low fertility needs
- 100 plants per sq m
- 7kg (15½lb) per sq m

Recommended varieties

Mixed lettuce packs, 'All the Year Round', 'Freckles', 'Little Gem', 'Amaze', 'Bronze Beauty' (bolt resistant)

Growing

Lettuce is quick to grow, and even a small patch provides a significant quantity of food. All lettuces can be treated as cut-and-come-again for leaves, but some (such as 'Little Gem') will develop heads. Grow varieties to suit what you need in the kitchen.

STAGE 1

Using a rake handle, make rows 1cm (½in) deep, with 10cm (4in) between rows. **Sow** 1 seed every 1cm (½in). Cover each row with soil, pat down firmly, and **water** well.

STAGE 2

If warm and dry, **water** daily until seedlings germinate.

STAGE 3

When seedlings are 10cm (4in) tall, **thin** by carefully cutting at the base to avoid disturbing others in the row and to leave 1 strong lettuce seedling every 10cm (4in). Ideally do this over a few days as the thinnings will yield quite a lot of food.

CONTAINER GROWING

Sow seeds by scattering them on the surface, cover with 1cm (½in) of compost, and **water** in. **Thin** them as at stage 3.

HARVEST

There are two ways to harvest lettuce. You can cut-and-come-again by picking the biggest leaves first and allowing the smaller ones to mature, little but often. For a heading type, allow the plant to mature to harvest the whole head.

Look out for

A common issue is bolting. This is when leafy greens run to seed in dry conditions in an attempt to reproduce before dying back. The result is reduced yield. Prevent bolting by watering well in dry weather, and grow lettuce shaded by other plants such as corn or climbing beans. A selection of "slow-bolt" leafy varieties is available. Slugs may also damage lettuces (see p.107).

Cooking

🔪 CHARRED LETTUCE WITH LEMON AND TAHINI DRESSING

Lettuce is most often enjoyed fresh and crisp straight from the garden in a salad or sandwich, but here I wanted to share an alternative: warm and smoky, with a balanced lemon and tahini dressing.

Serves 2 as a side or starter

Ingredients

2 small, firm lettuces (such as cos, romaine, or 'Little Gem'), halved lengthways

60ml (2fl oz) olive oil

Pinch of sea salt

Toasted seeds (sunflower or sesame)

Sumac or chilli flakes (optional)

Fresh herbs (such as dill or parsley)

For the dressing

30g (1oz) tahini

2 tbsp lemon juice

1 tbsp honey

1 small garlic clove, grated

Freshly ground black pepper

1. Drizzle the lettuces lightly with olive oil and salt. Heat a griddle pan or cast-iron frying pan; when the pan is hot, place the lettuces cut-side down and cook until charred and starting to wilt at the edges. Flip and cook briefly on the other side.

2. Meanwhile, whisk together the tahini, lemon juice, honey, garlic, and a splash of cold water to loosen. The dressing should be silky and pourable. Season to taste.

3. Arrange the charred lettuce on a plate, drizzle with the dressing, and scatter with toasted seeds, spices (if using), and herbs.

Salad dressings

A helpful guide for salad dressing is to use 2 parts oil to 1 part vinegar.

Vinegar Red wine vinegar or balsamic complement olives, radicchio, mature cheeses, tomatoes, and beetroot, while pale vinegars like apple cider, sherry, or white wine vinegar suit root veg, grains, nuts, young cheeses, and sesame.

Oil Use an extra virgin olive oil for a rich peppery kick, and balance it with salt and honey or maple syrup.

Extras For a creative twist, add some fresh, gently bruised herbs, or citrus zest or juice.

Spinach

Key growing information

- Mid-spring to late summer
- 1cm (½in) sowing depth
- 10cm (4in) between plants
- 10 weeks to harvest
- Full sun and partial shade
- Hardy
- High water needs
- Low fertility needs
- 100 plants per sq m
- 4kg (9lb) per sq m

Recommended varieties

'Medania', 'Matador' (pictured right), 'Giant Winter'

Growing

A fast-growing leafy green, spinach thrives in cool conditions, performing best around the tail end of the growing season.

STAGE 1

Use a rake handle to make shallow drills spaced 10cm (4in) apart in your garden bed. **Sow** 1 seed every centimetre (½in), and cover the drill with soil, gently pat down, and **water** thoroughly.

STAGE 2

Water during warm, dry weather, daily if needed, to ensure strong germination.

STAGE 3

Once seedlings are around 10cm (4in) tall, **thin** to either 1 plant every 10cm (4in) for larger leaves, or every 5cm (2in) for baby spinach. You can eat the thinnings.

CONTAINER GROWING

Sow 1 seed every 2–3cm (1in) on the surface and cover with compost, watering in well afterwards. **Thin** to 1 seedling every 5cm (2in).

HARVEST

Pick leaves with your fingers, aiming to keep as much stem as possible with the leaf. Pick a maximum of 2 or 3 leaves at a time from each plant to ensure continuous leaf production. Taking too many at a time will slow down how quickly the plant can create new leaves.

Look out for

Leaf miner (see p.140) and bolting (see p.142) can affect spinach.

Cooking

🍳 ALOO PALAK

This version of aloo palak (spinach and potato curry), a much-loved North Indian dish, has been gently adjusted for ease and accessibility, while staying true to the earthy, spiced character that defines it. Tender potatoes and silky spinach are simmered in a fragrant blend of cumin, turmeric, and garam masala. It's comforting, deeply savoury, and simple to make with fresh garden produce.

Serves 4

Ingredients

1½ tbsp oil (sunflower or vegetable)

1 tsp cumin seeds

1 large onion, finely chopped

3 garlic cloves, grated

1 thumb-sized piece of ginger, grated

1 green chilli (optional), finely chopped

1 tsp ground coriander

½ tsp ground turmeric

1 tsp garam masala

½ tsp chilli powder (optional)

500g (1lb 2oz) floury potatoes, peeled and cubed

100ml (3½fl oz) water

½ tsp sea salt, or to taste

400g (14oz) fresh spinach, washed and roughly chopped

Juice of ½ lemon

1. Heat the oil on a medium heat in a wide pan and add the cumin seeds. Once they begin to sizzle, stir in the chopped onion and cook until golden.

2. Add the garlic, ginger, and green chilli, and sauté until fragrant. Stir in the ground coriander, turmeric, garam masala, and chilli powder. Fry briefly to bloom the spices.

3. Add the cubed potatoes, water, and salt. Cover and leave to simmer on a medium–low heat, stirring occasionally, until the potatoes are tender.

4. Stir in the spinach and cook, uncovered, until it's wilted and well combined. Finish with lemon juice and season to taste. Serve with chapatis or rice.

Tip
Leftovers make an excellent pasty filling the next day: simply mash lightly, fill the pastry, and bake.

Alternative recipe
For those wishing to explore a more traditional flavour profile, you can substitute a few of the ingredients with more regional items. Instead of lemon juice, use 1 teaspoon amchur (dried mango powder), and instead of neutral oil use mustard oil for depth. You can also add a pinch of asafoetida (hing) with the cumin seeds.

Chicory

Key growing information

- Late spring to late summer
- 1cm (½in) sowing depth
- 25cm (10in) between plants
- 12–14 weeks to harvest
- Full sun and partial shade
- Hardy
- Medium water needs
- Medium fertility needs
- 16 plants per sq m
- 5kg (11lb) per sq m

Recommended varieties

'Palla Rossa', 'Rossa di Treviso', 'Sugar Loaf'

Growing

STAGE 1

Sowing direct
Make shallow drills 10cm (4in) apart. **Sow** 1 seed every 1cm (½in), cover, and **water**.

Sowing in modules
Sow 2 per cell under cover. **Thin** to the strongest.

STAGE 2

When sown direct
Thin at 10cm (4in) tall.

When sown in modules
Plant out when seedlings have 4 or 5 true leaves.

CONTAINER GROWING
Plant seedlings at 20cm (8in)

HARVEST
Cut with a knife at the base.

Cooking

PAN-FRIED CHICORY

Serves 2

Ingredients

4 heads of chicory (red or white), halved lengthways

2 tbsp neutral oil (such as sunflower or light olive oil)

Juice of ½ orange

1 tbsp soy sauce

2 tsp honey or maple syrup

2 tsp rice vinegar or white wine vinegar

Toasted sesame seeds or crushed walnuts (to garnish)

Finely sliced spring onion or grated orange zest (optional)

1. Heat the oil in a frying pan over a medium–high heat. Place the chicory halves cut-side down and sear for 3–4 minutes, until golden and slightly softened. Cook briefly on the other side.

2. Meanwhile, whisk together the orange juice, soy sauce, honey (or syrup), and vinegar. Pour this glaze into the pan and reduce the heat to a gentle simmer.

3. Turn the chicory to coat, cooking for 2–3 minutes until the glaze thickens and clings.

4. Plate the chicory with the sauce spooned over, and garnish. Serve warm.

Endive

Key growing information

- Early to late summer
- 1cm (½in) sowing depth
- 25cm (10in) between plants
- 10 weeks to harvest
- Full sun and partial shade
- Hardy
- Medium water needs
- Medium fertility needs
- 16 plants per sq m
- 4kg (9lb) per sq m

Recommended varieties

'Bianca Riccia da Taglio', 'Pancalieri', 'En Cornet De Bordeaux'

Growing

STAGE 1
Sow 2 seeds per module cell under cover.

STAGE 2
Thin to the strongest.

STAGE 3
Plant out when seedlings have 4 or 5 true leaves.
Water in warm, dry weather.

CONTAINER GROWING
Space seedlings (stage 3) 25cm (10in) apart.

HARVEST
Harvest 2 or 3 outer leaves per plant, pulling them down away from the centre.

Look out for
Slugs (see p.107).

Cooking

ENDIVE AND PEAR WINTER SALAD

Serves 2 as a starter or light lunch

Ingredients

2 heads endive, trimmed and leaves separated

1 ripe pear, thinly sliced

Small handful of toasted hazelnuts, roughly chopped

30–40g (1–1½oz) blue cheese or goat's cheese, crumbled

A few radicchio or frisée leaves for colour (optional)

For the dressing

1 tbsp olive oil

1 tbsp cider vinegar

1 tbsp Dijon mustard

1 tbsp honey

Sea salt and freshly ground black pepper, to taste

1. Whisk the oil, vinegar, mustard, honey, salt, and pepper to make a dressing.

2. Toss the endive and pear with the dressing.

3. Place on a serving dish and scatter with hazelnuts and cheese. Serve straight away.

Rocket

Key growing information

- Mid-spring to early autumn
- 1cm (½in) sowing depth
- 10cm (4in) between plants
- 6 weeks to harvest
- Full sun and partial shade
- Hardy
- High water needs
- Low fertility needs
- 100 plants per sq m
- 3kg (6½lb) per sq m

Recommended varieties

'Astra', 'Dragon's Fire', wild rocket

Growing

STAGE 1
Sow 1 seed every 1cm (½in), cover with soil, and **water** well.

STAGE 2
A week after germination, **thin** to their final spacing.

STAGE 3
Continue to **water** well to prevent bolting (see p.142).

CONTAINER GROWING
Sow seeds by scattering them on the surface, cover, and keep watered. **Thin** once the seedlings emerge.

HARVEST
Pick leaves from the edges, taking no more than one-third at a time from a plant.

Cooking

ROCKET CRÊPES
Serves 2 (makes 4 crêpes)

Ingredients

2 large eggs

120ml (4fl oz) milk

60g (2oz) plain flour

Pinch of sea salt

Oil or butter for frying

50g (1¾oz) rocket

Mixed roasted vegetables from the garden (such as aubergine, pepper, onion)

100g (3½oz) feta, crumbled

2 tsp harissa

1. Whisk the eggs, milk, flour, and salt until smooth. Rest the mixture for 10 minutes while you heat a frying pan with oil.

2. Pour in a ladleful of batter, swirl, and top with a ripped handful of rocket while it cooks until golden (1–2 minutes). Flip and briefly cook the other side after 1 minute, pressing the rocket flat with the back of a spatula. Repeat until you run out of batter.

3. Fill each warm crêpe with roasted vegetables, feta, and a drizzle of harissa. Fold and serve hot.

Tip
You can swap the rocket for mustard greens.

Mustard

Key growing information

- 🌱 Mid-spring to early autumn
- ↕ 1cm (½in) sowing depth
- ↔ 15cm (6in) between plants
- 📅 6 weeks to harvest
- ☀ Full sun and partial shade
- ❄ Hardy
- 💧 High water needs
- 🌿 Low fertility needs
- ☐ 100 plants per sq m
- 🧺 3kg (6½lb) per sq m

Recommended varieties

'Wasabi', 'Red Giant', 'Red Frills', 'Golden Streaks'

Growing

STAGE 1
Sow 1 seed every 1cm (½in), cover with soil, and water well.

STAGE 2
Thin to their final spacing 2 weeks after germination.

STAGE 3
Keep **watering** to support the rapid rate of growth and prevent bolting (see p.142).

CONTAINER GROWING
Sow seeds by scattering them on the surface, cover, and **water**. **Thin** seedlings.

HARVEST
Harvest 2 or 3 leaves per plant, pulling them away from the base.

Cooking

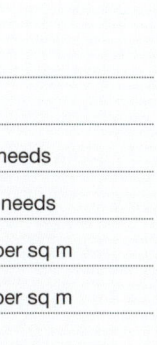 **MUSTARD LEAF SALAD**

Serves 2

Ingredients
100–150g (3½–5½oz) soft goat's cheese log, cut into 1cm (½in) rounds

2–4 slices of good-quality sourdough or rye bread

1–2 tsp runny honey

2 large handfuls of mustard leaves (green or red)

2 large handfuls of mixed salad leaves, rinsed and dried

1 small handful dried raisins and chopped dried apricots

1 small handful of walnuts or pecans

For the dressing
3 tbsp olive oil

1 tsp apple cider or white wine vinegar

1 tsp Dijon mustard

Pinch of sea salt

1. Preheat the oven to 200°C (180°C fan/400°F/Gas 6). Bake the cheese on the bread with a drizzle of honey for 8–10 minutes.

2. Tear the leaves and mix in the dried fruit.

3. Toast the walnuts in a dry pan, then roughly chop.

4. Add the dressing and nuts to the salad, then top with the cheese toasts.

Herbs

How to Grow Annual Herbs

Small but mighty, these herbs bring a whole new dimension of flavour to the kitchen garden. One of the best things about annual herbs is that, due to their strong flavour, they are less likely to experience slug damage. First, let's look at how to grow annual herbs direct, in modules, or in containers. Then, there is specific information on growing and harvesting four of our favourites; see pp.154–55.

STAGE 1
Sowing direct
Use the handle of a rake to make shallow drills 1cm (½in) deep. **Sow** 1 seed about every 1cm (½in), cover over with soil, pat down gently, and **water** well.

Sowing in modules
Sow 5–6 seeds per module cell, **water**, and don't let the compost dry out.

STAGE 2
When sown direct
Around a week after seeds have germinated, **thin** to 1 plant every 7–10cm (3–4in); these single plants are closer together than the recommended spacing for clumps (see pp.154–55).

When sown in modules
Once seedlings have emerged, use snips to **thin** them to 3 or 4 plants per cell.

STAGE 3
When sown direct
Around 2 weeks after thinning, weed between the rows to reduce competition for water and nutrients. This will allow the herb seedlings to take off and smother any future weed competition.

When sown in modules
Once each seedling has 3 or 4 true leaves, **plant out** each clump to the recommended spacing (see pp.154–55). Use your fingers or a trowel to make a hole the size of the rootball, firmly press the rootball into the hole, and water thoroughly.

CONTAINER GROWING
Lightly **sow** seeds on the compost surface, 1–2cm (½–¾in) apart, cover with 1cm (½in) of compost, and **water** in. After germination, **thin** to 1 every 7–10cm (3–4in) and keep watered, particularly on hot days.

Herbs

CORIANDER
Key growing information

- 🌱 Mid-spring to late summer
- ↕ 1cm (½in) sowing depth
- ↔ 15cm (6in) between clumps
- 📅 8 weeks to harvest
- ☀ Full sun and partial shade
- ❄ Half hardy (will survive light frost)
- 💧 High water needs
- 🌿 Medium fertility needs
- ☐ 36 (clumps) per sq m
- 🧺 1–2kg (2¼–5¼lb) per sq m

Recommended varieties
'Slow Bolt', 'Confetti', 'Calypso', 'Leafy Leisure'

Coriander (pictured above and on p.153) offers a bold, citrusy punch and is either loved or hated by taste buds. While it's quick to bolt, or run to seed (see p.142), the edible flowers make a great food source for pollinators, and then produce green seeds, which can be used fresh or dried. **Sow** every 4 weeks for a continuous leaf supply since it is so prone to running to seed. **Harvest** leaves often by pinching off stems from the base of the plant, taking no more than one-third at a time.

BASIL
Key growing information

- 🌱 Mid-spring to midsummer
- ↕ 1cm (½in) sowing depth
- ↔ 15cm (6in) between clumps of plants
- 📅 10 weeks to harvest
- ☀ Full sun and partial shade
- ❄ Tender
- 💧 Medium water needs
- 🌿 Low fertility needs
- ☐ 36 (clumps) per sq m
- 🧺 1–2kg (2¼–5¼lb) per sq m

Recommended varieties
'British', 'Genovese', 'Sweet Basil', 'Lettuce Leaf Basil'

A warmth-loving herb, basil (pictured below) is best grown under cover. It's known for its perfect pairing with tomatoes in the kitchen, and this can also apply in the garden where many growers have basil under their tomato plants. **Harvest** 1 or 2 sprigs of leaves at a time per plant, taking growth from the top to encourage the plant to bush out. Look out for bolting (see p.142), and if you see flower spikes, pinch them off to prolong harvests.

How to Grow Annual Herbs

PARSLEY
Key growing information

- Mid-spring to midsummer
- 1cm (½in) sowing depth
- 25cm (10in) between clumps
- 12 weeks to harvest
- Full sun and partial shade
- Hardy
- Medium water needs
- Low fertility needs
- 16 (clumps) per sq m
- 1–2kg (2¼–5¼lb) per sq m

Recommended varieties
'Italian Giant', 'Plain Leaf', 'Triple Curled'

Parsley (pictured above) is a versatile staple, offering plenty of leaves over a long harvest period. It takes an extra week or two to germinate compared to the other annual herbs here.

To **harvest**, cut outer stems from the base to allow smaller central stems to continue growing. Take no more than one-quarter of the stems at a time. Parsley can be overwintered outside for winter leaves and fresh growth the following season before it starts flowering in mid-spring, which is a great time to sow a fresh batch.

DILL
Key growing information

- Mid-spring to late summer
- 1cm (½in) sowing depth
- 15cm (6in) between clumps
- 8 weeks to harvest
- Full sun and partial shade
- Half hardy (will survive light frost)
- Medium water needs
- Low fertility needs
- 36 (clumps) per sq m
- 1–2kg (2¼–5¼lb) per sq m

Recommended varieties
'Bouquet', 'Mammoth', 'Hera'

A feathery and delicate herb that can be mistaken for fennel seedlings when young, dill (pictured below) is a cool-loving and rapid-growing herb with leaves loved by chefs, and flowers adored by pollinators. **Harvest** the top 10cm (4in) of the dill plant by pinching out to encourage it to send up more feathery leafy tops to pick at a later date. Look out for bolting (see p.142).

How to Grow Perennial Herbs

Perennial herbs are a must in any garden, even if you simply grow a few in a large container. In addition to their kitchen uses, they offer incredible benefits to pollinators, with long flowering periods and flowers that are easily accessible for both nectar and pollen.

Some perennial herbs, such as thyme and rosemary, like drier soil, while others, such as mint and lemon balm, thrive in wetter conditions. Aim to grow herbs with similar needs together so they are easier to manage, though almost all of these herbs are hands-off, apart from their watering needs.

When purchasing herb plants, choose those grown in 9cm (3½in) pots as these tend to be most cost-effective and will mature quickly once planted.

To **plant out** a pot-grown herb, create a hole slightly deeper than the plant. Add a handful of compost and mix with the soil at the base. Remove the plant from the pot, place it in the hole, **water** well and push the soil around the rootball. The plant should be at the same level as it was in its pot.

Mulch around the plant with a 15–20cm (6–8in) radius of straw, grass, or similar, 5cm (2in) deep, to help retain moisture and keep it free of weeds while it establishes.

In the profiles on the following pages we've provided specific harvesting advice for each herb, and recommended types that offer unique characteristics. Lemon verbena, for example (see p.160), has an amazing variety that offers a potent ginger scent. These choices give you so much creativity when it comes to using perennial herbs in your cooking, offering you fresh flavours that money simply can't buy!

THYME
Key growing information

- ↔ 30cm (12in) between plants
- 🗓 Harvest all year round
- ☼ Full sun
- ❄ Hardy
- 💧 Low water needs
- 🜂 Low fertility needs

Recommended varieties
Lemon, broad leaf, creeping

Thyme (pictured above) is a small yet powerful herb, slow growing and with a low profile, but it will in time form a thick ground cover. This makes it ideal for positioning under and in front of taller herbs such as rosemary. While harvests are year-round, the best flavour and leaf quality is just before flowering in summer. **Snip** sprigs as needed, or use some shears to give the plant a bit of a haircut as this will also encourage strong regrowth. The tiny pink and purple flowers are edible, and loved by pollinators.

ROSEMARY
Key growing information

- ↔ 60cm (24in) between plants
- 🗓 Harvest all year round
- ☼ Full sun
- ❄ Hardy
- 💧 Low water needs
- 🜂 Low fertility needs

Recommended varieties
Common and trailing rosemary, 'Barbecue'

Rosemary (pictured right) has a strong pine-like aroma, with needle-shaped leaves coming off the tall stems. In spring it produces pale purple edible flowers, with a noticeable rosemary flavour. In the right place, rosemary can turn into a small shrub, up to 150cm (5ft) high and 120cm (4ft) wide. A great location to plant rosemary is towards the back of a sunny border. Frequent harvesting will help maintain vigour. **Harvest** sprigs whenever needed: the greener the stem, the less bitter the flavours if you are using whole sprigs for roasts.

SAGE

Key growing information

- ↔ 30cm (12in) between plants
- 📅 Harvest all year round
- ☀ Full sun
- ❄ Hardy
- 💧 Low water needs
- 🌱 Low fertility needs

Recommended varieties
Common, purple, and blackcurrant sage

An evergreen and woody perennial, sage (pictured below) makes small bushes of grey-green leaves that have a soft texture. **Cut** whole stems or pick individual leaves as needed, though focus on leaves over the winter to maintain plant health. Freshen up plants every spring by cutting back old stems by one-third to just above a leaf or node; avoid pruning in autumn.

OREGANO

Key growing information

- ↔ 40cm (16in) between plants
- 📅 Harvest mid-spring to mid-autumn
- ☀ Full sun and partial shade
- ❄ Hardy
- 💧 Low water needs
- 🌱 Low fertility needs

Recommended varieties
Common and golden oregano, 'Hot & Spicy'

A vigorous soft-stemmed plant, oregano (pictured above) forms a dense clump of leafy stems. The flowers are a favourite for bumblebees. In late winter, cut back the dead woody growth to ground level and use this material to mulch the "crown" from where the stems appear, helping to protect the plant from cold weather. **Harvest** stems of the plant as you need, cutting just above a pair of leaves to encourage strong regrowth.

Tip
French marjoram is a cousin of oregano, but has a milder and sweeter taste. It is grown and harvested in the same way.

How to Grow Perennial Herbs

CHIVES

Key growing information

- ↔ 25cm (10in) between plants
- 🗓 Harvest early spring to late summer
- ☀ Full sun and partial shade
- ❄ Hardy
- 💧 Medium water needs
- 🌱 Medium fertility needs

Recommended varieties
Common and garlic chives, 'White One'

One of the easiest and most useful herbs for a kitchen garden, chives (pictured above) are among the first of any perennials to emerge in spring. The pom-pom-like blooms are a bit of a showstopper, and you can easily divide chive clumps to create more. Once they have had their first flush of flowers, cut them back at the base to get a second flush of greens in the same growing season. **Harvest** leaves as needed by cutting at the base of the plant; for flowers, which make a great edible garnish, gently snap them off with a little stem attached.

MINT

Key growing information

- ↔ 50cm (20in) between plants
- 🗓 Harvest mid-spring to mid-autumn
- ☀ Full sun and partial shade
- ❄ Hardy
- 💧 High water needs
- 🌱 Medium fertility needs

Recommended varieties
Moroccan, apple, and Thai mint

Be warned: mint will do anything it can to take over, so it's a good idea to restrict it by growing it in a large pot. Mint needs a lot of water, particularly if growing in containers, so consider placing your mint in partial shade to reduce evaporation. The aroma of fresh mint is somewhat addictive, so enjoy it as much as possible: **harvest** leaves or whole stems at the base as needed. It dies back each winter, re-emerging the following spring. In the same way as for oregano (see opposite), cut back the woody dead growth.

Herbs

LEMON VERBENA
Key growing information

- ↔ 60cm (24in) between plants
- ▦ Harvest mid-spring to early autumn
- ☀ Full sun
- ❋ Half hardy
- ◊ Low water needs
- ⌀ Medium fertility needs

Recommended varieties
Lemon, ginger

Imagine growing a plant that smells like sherbet – well you can! Lemon verbena (pictured above) has such an intense lemon scent that you can't help but grab a leaf to crush when you pass by. It grows as a small wispy shrub with delicate leaves and airy stems. Unlike the other herbs featured, lemon verbena is susceptible to cold, so plant it in a polytunnel, or in a container outside which can be brought in during cold spells. **Harvest** leaves as needed, or cut a whole stem to dry and preserve its fragrance.

LEMON BALM
Key growing information

- ↔ 75cm (30in) between plants
- ▦ Harvest mid-spring to early autumn
- ☀ Full sun and partial shade
- ❋ Hardy
- ◊ High water needs
- ⌀ Medium fertility needs

Recommended varieties
Lemon, lime, orange

Lemon balm (pictured below) is a fast-growing, bushy herb that can form large clumps which create a gentle feel to borders. The crinkly leaves yield a citrus scent when crushed, and although the flowers are tiny, they offer pollinator benefits. **Cut** stems or growing tips as needed, or **pick** individual leaves. The quality of the leaf flavour declines after flowering, so consider cutting right back for fresh growth. In winter cut back all the dead stems to the base so next year's growth doesn't get tangled.

How to Grow Perennial Herbs

LAVENDER
Key growing information

- ↔ 45cm (18in) between plants
- 🗓 Early to late summer (flowers)
- ☀ Full sun
- ❄ Hardy
- 💧 Low water needs
- 🍃 Low fertility needs

Recommended varieties
'Hidcote', 'Beechwood Blue', 'Alba'

Lavender (pictured above) is an absolute joy for your eyes and nose as well as for pollinators. It is also the fussiest of the herbs, and hates sitting in wet soil over winter, so place it where there is excellent drainage.

Lavender forms an evergreen micro-bush, and produces beautiful flowers with a powerful scent. For the best drying quality, **cut** flower stems just as the buds begin to open. Lightly cut back one-third of new growth after the flowers have faded to help keep the bush compact and vibrant.

AGASTACHE
Key growing information

- ↔ 50cm (20in) between plants
- 🗓 Harvest mid-spring to mid-autumn
- ☀ Full sun
- ❄ Hardy
- 💧 Low water needs
- 🍃 Medium fertility needs

Recommended varieties
Korean mint, hyssop, 'Blackadder'

A favourite of ours, agastache (pictured below) is a stunning herb with great kitchen uses. The shrubby habit and tall purple flower spikes make it unmissable to humans and bees, and it is often planted as an easier-to-grow lavender alternative for impressive borders. One species, *Agastache rugosa*, is commonly known as Korean mint and is our preference when it comes to food and drink. Pick leaves and flower spikes when needed, or harvest entire stems if you are after greater volume. Cut back dead growth over winter for healthy regrowth.

Cooking with Herbs

Herbs offer a wide variety of character and aroma to dishes, whether used fresh from the garden, dried, or infused in vinegar, oil, or butter. Fresh herbs in particular carry the fleeting flavours of the garden while they are at their most fragrant and vibrant. On the following pages is a selection of recipes that use herbs to flavour butter, oil, tea, sugar, and salt (see pp.164–67), followed by some feature recipes in which herbs are the star (see pp.168–69).

In the kitchen, herbs are categorized as soft or hard. Broadly speaking, to make the most of soft herbs like basil and parsley, they should be added right before serving, after the cooking process has finished, so that they can retain their delicate aromatic qualities. Hard herbs, such as thyme and rosemary, are more robust, and require a more prolonged, gentle heat to make the most of their flavour.

FRESH HERBS
Hard herbs in the kitchen
These garden staples include rosemary, thyme, oregano, sage, marjoram, and bay. All add depth to your food when exposed to heat, and handle being cooked very well. Strip the leaves from the woody stem and scatter them over roast veg, grilled cheese, or fried eggs. Stir into butter or oil for an instant flavour boost. Infuse in hot water for a soothing herbal tea, or toss sprigs into stews, broths, or pan sauces to lift them with fragrant brightness. Mix with lemon zest and salt for a quick rub for meat or mushrooms. Add to marinades, salad dressings, or even honey for a savoury twist. Hard herbs like thyme and rosemary also infuse well in spirits for herbal notes in cocktails.

Soft herbs in the kitchen
Soft herbs include parsley, basil, coriander, dill,

Cooking with Herbs

tarragon, chervil, lemon balm, and lemon verbena. Used fresh, these herbs offer brightness to dishes, but should be added like a finishing salt as extended cooking dulls or destroys their aroma. Stir chopped leaves into gnocchi, stuffings, savoury scones, salads, or roast potatoes, where they complement both summer and autumn flavours such as chestnut, apple, and brown butter.

DRIED HERBS
To preserve homegrown herbs for year-round flavour, harvest just before flowering, when the oils are at their strongest. Pick in the morning after the dew has dried.

Drying hard herbs
Straight after picking, tie the stems into small bundles to hang upside down in a warm, dry, well-ventilated place out of direct sunlight. Once leaves are crisp (1–2 weeks), strip them and store in airtight jars away from heat and light. You can also dry leaves in a dehydrator or low oven (below 40°C/104°F, or fan only) for a few hours. This method works beautifully for thyme, rosemary, marjoram, and savory, and fills your kitchen with frugal, flavoursome, dried herbs straight from your garden.

Drying soft herbs
To dry soft herbs, you'll get better results using a dehydrator or fan oven with the temperature set to below 30°C (85°F) for 8–10 hours. This method preserves a much better flavour than hanging, which tends to favour hard herbs.

Herbs

🧈 HERB COMPOUND BUTTER

Compound butter is a fancy way of saying butter mixed with another flavour. Fats capture and elevate fragrant ingredients. With their abundance of aromatic qualities, herbs lend themselves beautifully to making bespoke compound butters from your garden.

Compound butter is perfect melted over new potatoes, steamed fish, roasted carrots, or grilled corn, or folded into scrambled eggs. It's also excellent as a finishing touch for soups or spread inside a sandwich with pickled vegetables. Adding miso to the butter gives an umami element. It not only enhances the savouriness but also balances the freshness of the herbs with a subtle, fermented richness.

Ingredients

250g (9oz) unsalted butter

Large handful of fresh herbs, finely chopped (including tender stems, but remove woody ones)

Sea salt

1 tsp red or white miso (optional)

1. Soften the butter at room temperature until it's easily spreadable.

2. Mix the chopped herbs thoroughly into the butter with a good pinch of sea salt. Stir in white or red miso, if using. Spoon the combined butter onto a sheet of baking paper and roll into a log. Twist the ends to seal, and chill until firm. You can also shape it into ramekins or freeze in spoonfuls for easy use. Stored in the fridge, it will keep for up to a week. Frozen, it can last for 3–6 months.

Alternative recipes

Other creative pairings include: roasted garlic and preserved lemon; anchovy and parsley; chives, mustard leaves, and wild garlic; or thyme and yeast extract.

HERB OIL

Vibrant, aromatic, and surprisingly versatile, herb oil is a great way to preserve fresh herbs for multiple uses in the kitchen. You can use this method with parsley for green notes and mild bitterness, coriander for a citrusy kick, basil for Italian dishes, wild garlic for vernal spice, or chives for a mild allium note. Use herb oil to finish soups, drizzle over grilled vegetables, swirl into hummus, or spoon onto fish or eggs for a fresh, herbal lift.

Ingredients
Large bunch of fresh herbs

150ml (5fl oz) neutral oil, such as grapeseed, sunflower, or light olive oil

1. Blanch the fresh herbs in boiling water for about 10 seconds, just until the leaves turn bright green. Immediately transfer to a bowl of ice water to halt the cooking and preserve the colour. Drain and dry thoroughly using a clean tea towel or salad spinner.

2. Add the herbs to a blender with the oil. Blend on high for 1–2 minutes until the mixture is smooth and vibrantly green.

3. Strain through a fine mesh sieve, muslin cloth, or coffee filter to remove solids. Pour the clear green oil into a sterilized jar or bottle (see p.28).

4. Store in the fridge for up to 1 week, or freeze in ice cube trays for up to 3 months.

PICKLING HERBS

This is a quick way to capture herbs' freshness in a tangy, versatile way. Pack sprigs into a clean jar or bottle and cover with vinegar (hot for hard herbs, or cold for soft herbs). Cover and leave ambient for a week before using. It will last for months if the herbs stay below the vinegar's surface.

HERB SALT

A fragrant, easy way to preserve a fresh herbal aroma, herb salt (pictured below) adds punch to roasted vegetables, grilled meats, or even the rim of a cocktail glass. This method works brilliantly with parsley, dill, basil, tarragon, sage, wild garlic, coriander, lemon zest, or even dried chilli. Try mixing and matching, such as thyme (see p.157) with lemon, or rosemary (see p.157) with smoked salt, for custom seasoning blends.

Ingredients

100g (3½oz) fresh herbs (leaves and tender stems)

100g (3½oz) coarse sea salt

1. Blend the fresh herbs with the sea salt until you have a vivid green, damp mixture.

2. Spread this out thinly on a baking tray lined with parchment, and dry in front of a fan or open window for 12–24 hours, or until completely dry and crisp. Stir occasionally to help the mixture dry evenly.

3. Once cool, blitz again to a fine, even salt and store in an airtight jar at room temperature for up to 6 months.

Tip

For the best colour and brighter flavour, you can freeze this mixture instead of drying it. Blend the herbs and salt as above, spoon into a small container, and freeze. It won't be dry, but it keeps the vivid green and is perfect for adding to sauces or marinades straight from the freezer.

HERB SUGAR

Often deeply fragrant and floral, this aromatic sugar is perfect for sweetening shortbread, cakes, scones, or herbal teas. A little goes a long way as it can add a potent fragrance, so start with small amounts. Herbs that work well are lavender, chamomile, elderflower, rosemary, thyme, sage, mint, lemon verbena, and lemon balm. Use just the flowers if you want to preserve colour, but add leaves if you want to make the most of the plant. For variation, try adding lemon zest, vanilla bean, or rose petals for a more complex floral sugar blend.

Ingredients

1 tbsp floral herbs, such as lavender buds

200g (7oz) granulated or caster sugar

1. Combine the herbs with the sugar. Pulse briefly in a food processor for a finer texture, or simply stir together for a more rustic mix.

2. Store in an airtight jar for at least 2 days before using, allowing the flavour to infuse. Once made, it keeps for several months.

HERBAL TEAS

Tea made from leaves changes dramatically depending on whether it's kept fresh or allowed to oxidize. Fresh teas (like green tea or mint) are bright, grassy, and close to the living plant, full of fleeting citrus and floral or menthol notes. Oxidized teas (like black tea, bruised sage, or raspberry leaf) trade that sharpness for deeper flavours of honey, dried fruit, or even spice, with more body and tannin.

Fresh mint tea

Fragrant, cooling, and calming, mint tea is perfect hot or chilled. Other herbs that work beautifully as a fresh tea are lavender, rosemary, sage, lemon balm, lemon verbena, fennel leaf, basil, and raspberry leaf.

To make the tea, rinse a small handful of fresh mint leaves (any variety), and gently bruise them to release their oils. Place them in a teapot or mug and pour over water heated to around 90°C (194°F) (just below boiling). Steep for 5–7 minutes, covered, to trap the aromatics. For a stronger flavour, steep for up to 10 minutes and don't be afraid to use lots of mint.

Strain and serve hot, or chill over ice for iced mint tea. Add a slice of lemon, a drizzle of honey, or a few sprigs of lemon balm for variation. This tea is best enjoyed fresh, but can be refrigerated for a day.

Oxidized lemon verbena tea

Lemon verbena makes a rich, smooth, and deeply aromatic tea. Other plants that work well as oxidized teas are raspberry leaf (see p.177), blackberry leaf, strawberry leaf, apple leaf, currant leaf, sage, thyme, and rose leaf.

Harvest fresh lemon verbena leaves and gently bruise or roll them between your palms to break the cell walls. Place the leaves in a clean, breathable container (such as a wooden bowl or basket), cover loosely with a cloth, and leave them to oxidize at room temperature for 24–36 hours, until they darken and develop a fruity, floral aroma. During this time, mix them twice a day, then dry the leaves in a dehydrator or low oven (around 40°C/104°F) until crisp. Store in an airtight jar.

To brew, steep in hot water (90°C/194°F) for 5–7 minutes or to taste.

CHIVE AND OAT CRACKERS

These crackers are great with cheese, dips, or on their own. Instead of chives you can use sage, parsley, rosemary, or thyme.

Makes about 20 small crackers

Ingredients

100g (3½oz) rolled oats

50g (1¾oz) plain flour

½ tsp sea salt

1 tbsp fresh chives, chopped

2 tbsp olive oil

1. Preheat the oven to 180°C (160°C fan/350°F/Gas 4). Line a baking tray.

2. In a bowl, mix the oats, flour, salt, and chives. Add the olive oil and 4–5 tbsp water gradually, stirring until a firm dough forms.

3. Roll out the dough thinly between 2 sheets of baking paper. Cut it into squares and place them on the lined tray.

4. Bake for 15–18 minutes until crisp and golden. Cool completely before storing in an airtight tin.

ROSEMARY AND OLIVE SCONES

Nothing beats a savoury scone (pictured above). Buttery, tender, and flecked with rosemary, it's perfect with soup or cheese, or just warm with a little butter.

Makes 6–8 scones

Ingredients

50g (1¾oz) cold butter, cubed

225g (8oz) self-raising flour

½ tsp baking powder

1 tbsp fresh rosemary, finely chopped

75g (2½oz) black olives, chopped

Pinch of sea salt

120ml (4fl oz) milk (plus extra for brushing)

1. Preheat the oven to 200°C (180°C fan/400°F/Gas 6). Rub the butter into the flour and baking powder until the mixture resembles breadcrumbs, then stir in the rosemary, olives, and salt.

2. Add milk gradually to form a soft dough, then roll it out to 2–3cm (1in) thick and cut into rounds.

3. Line a baking tray with parchment, then place the scones on the tray, brush with milk, and bake for 12–15 minutes until golden. Serve warm with butter and cheese.

Cooking with Herbs

🫙 BASIL PESTO

A homemade pesto couldn't be simpler to make. This recipe works with traditional cheeses or as a plant-based version. Homemade pesto captures the essence of summer, and brings green vitality to almost any dish.

Makes 1 small jar

Ingredients

50g (1¾oz) fresh basil leaves

30g (1oz) pine nuts

1 garlic clove, grated

30g (1oz) Parmesan or pecorino cheese, grated, or 1 tbsp nutritional yeast

100ml (3½oz) good-quality olive oil, plus extra to cover

Lemon juice (to taste)

Pinch of sea salt

1. To make a classic basil pesto, blend the basil, pine nuts, garlic, cheese (or nutritional yeast for the vegan version) and olive oil. Add a squeeze of lemon juice and a pinch of salt to taste. Blitz until smooth or leave slightly textured, depending on preference.

2. Store in the fridge, topped with a thin layer of oil, for up to a week, or freeze in small portions for 3–6 months.

Meals with …

Pesto is far more than a pasta sauce. Here are some more ideas for how to use it in the kitchen.

Roast vegetables Loosen the pesto with a drizzle of olive oil and spoon over roast vegetables.

Soups Swirl into creamy or tomato soups.

Sandwiches Spread on sandwiches for a lemony herbal kick.

Fish or chicken Spoon onto grilled fish or chicken.

Lentils and potatoes Stir into warm lentils or new potatoes.

Dressing Use as a dressing base for tomato salads or grain bowls.

Alternative recipe

You can adapt the recipe for a garden glut: try wild garlic or rocket for bite, parsley or coriander for brightness, or blend multiple herbs for a layered flavour. Swap pine nuts for walnuts, sunflower seeds, or almonds.

Soft Fruit

Strawberry

Key growing information

- Early autumn or early spring
- 25cm (10in) between plants
- Harvest early to late summer
- Full sun and partial shade
- Hardy
- Medium water needs
- Medium fertility needs
- 16 plants per sq m
- 1–2kg (2¼–4½lb) per sq m

Recommended varieties

'Cambridge Favourite' (pictured right), 'Fennella', 'Buddy'

Growing

Arguably the most loved fruit, strawberries bring such joy in the smallest of spaces. Their low-growing, creeping habit means they can quickly spread, which makes them great for maximizing space by growing them under your other fruit bushes.

PLANTING

Plant strawberry plants, firm in, and **water** well.

MULCHING AND FEEDING

For the best quality fruits, **mulch** with straw, hay, or grass clippings in late spring so that the fruits rest on a "clean" surface rather than on the soil. This will help retain soil moisture for good fruit development, too. They will also benefit from a liquid feed (see p.13) at the start and end of spring.

PRUNING

At the end of summer, remove any "runners" coming off the main plant. Runners are long stems that grow from the parent plant and produce small, new plants. If these stems have rooted, the new plants can be transplanted or potted up. Every 3 years, compost the original plants and plant new ones from runners to maintain vigour.

CONTAINER GROWING

Strawberries are the most suitable fruit for containers, and can be planted closer together than in the ground as they will spill over. **Plant** 5 plants around the edge of a standard container, or space them 20cm (8in) apart for any other container.

HARVEST

Strawberries are ready to harvest when their skin has turned completely red. Harvest by gently pulling the fruits away from the plant.

Look out for

Once the first fruits begin ripening, use canes or pipes to create a support to throw over some netting to prevent blackbirds eating your crop. Weigh down the edges of the netting and ensure there are no gaps where the birds can get through and into the patch. Check daily to ensure no birds are trapped in the netting. Slugs can also be troublesome (see p.107).

Cooking

Strawberries come in all shapes and sizes. Hidden beneath a carpet of leaves, they are ruby-red, and freckled with seeds, with a scent that drifts through the air like no other. When you bite into one you get the perfect balance of bright acidity and soft sweetness, and a juice that speaks of rain and sun in equal measure.

STRAWBERRY JAM

To capture this berry in a perfectly set jam, begin with a mix of firm, ripe, and slightly under-ripe berries (the less ripe ones contain more natural pectin, which helps with setting). This recipe works for all soft fruits and berries, though timings, set, and sweetness may vary.

Makes about 4 x 250ml (9fl oz) jars

Ingredients

1kg (2¼lb) fresh strawberries, hulled

Juice of 1 lemon

800g (1¾lb) granulated sugar

1 grated tart apple (optional, for added pectin)

Equipment

4 x 250ml (9fl oz) jars, sterilized (see p.28)

Jam thermometer

1. Halve or quarter larger berries and mix in a large pan with lemon juice and sugar (and apple, if using). The lemon juice balances sweetness and boosts pectin. Let the mixture sit for 30 minutes to draw out the juices.

2. Place the pan over a low heat, stirring to dissolve the sugar before bringing to a steady boil. Skim off any foam. Boil rapidly, stirring often, until it reaches the setting point of 105°C (221°F) on a jam thermometer; this usually takes 15–25 minutes. If you don't have a thermometer, drop a spoonful on to a chilled plate and push it gently; if the surface of the jam wrinkles, it's ready.

3. Remove from the heat and rest for 5 minutes to prevent the fruit from floating. Ladle into warm, sterilized jars and seal immediately.

4. Store in a cool, dark place for up to a year and refrigerate after opening.

Meals with …

Your strawberry jam makes a great companion to savoury and sweet dishes.

Glaze for roast meats
Warm strawberry jam with a splash of balsamic vinegar and a pinch of black pepper makes a quick glaze that enhances pork chops, duck, or roast chicken.

Layered into grilled cheese Spread a thin layer inside a toasted cheese sandwich (especially with brie or sharp cheddar) for a sweet–savoury contrast.

Swirled into porridge or yoghurt Stir a spoonful through warm oats or thick yoghurt to add a taste of summer to breakfast.

Raspberry

Key growing information

- Late autumn to early winter or late winter to early spring
- 30cm (12in) between plants
- Harvest midsummer to mid-autumn
- Full sun
- Hardy
- Medium water needs
- Medium fertility needs
- 6–8 plants per sq m
- 1–1.5kg (2¼–3¼lb) per sq m

Recommended varieties

Summer fruiting 'Glen Coe', 'Glen Ample' (pictured right), 'Golden Everest'; **Autumn fruiting** 'Polka', 'Joan J', 'All Gold' (pictured far right); **Patio** 'Yummy'

Growing

Undemanding and resilient, raspberries are a wonderful soft fruit and are such a treat in themselves. Just be warned – once you have a raspberry patch it is a job to remove it! We only grow autumn-fruiting raspberries as they are less likely to be eaten by birds (see Look out for), and this also gives us a welcome soft fruit later in the season. In addition to being simpler to prune, autumn-fruiting canes don't require any support. While summer-fruiting raspberries need a little more care, growing both types extends your harvest season from midsummer to mid-autumn.

PLANTING

In beds or in the ground, mix in 5 or 6 generous spadefuls of well-rotted manure per square metre. **Plant** canes (single stems with roots) about 30cm (1ft) apart by using a spade to create a deep slit to push the roots into. Ensure there is around 5cm (2in) of stem depth in the ground, then use your foot to push soil around the stem. **Water** thoroughly.

MULCHING AND FEEDING

Every winter, **mulch** with a generous layer of 5–7cm (2–3in) of leaves, hay, grass, or well-rotted manure around your raspberry canes. There is no need to use a liquid feed – mulching with organic material will provide adequate nutrition over the long term.

PRUNING

Depending on which type of raspberries you grow, there are two main ways to prune. Raspberry prunings can be used at the base of your compost bins for air flow (see p.14), or just cut up roughly and laid on top of the raspberry patch.

Summer-fruiting

Summer-fruiting raspberries fruit on the second-year

Raspberry

canes (the previous year's growth), so do not prune them the winter after planting. Add simple support at this stage: four posts around the outside of the patch, with wire at about 1.2m (4ft) high to act as a little fence. After the second growing season, in early winter, carefully go through your raspberry patch and **cut back** all second-year canes to just above the ground. These can be identified as they have a noticeably darker stem, and usually have evidence of fruiting spurs on them.

Autumn-fruiting
Fruit appears on the stems that grow in the same season, making these plants much simpler to manage than summer raspberries. In early winter, simply **cut back** all the stems to just above ground level.

CONTAINER GROWING
Due to their growth habit, raspberries aren't suitable for growing in containers unless you opt for a dwarf or patio variety.

HARVEST
Gently pull ripe fruits away from the plant. They are ripe when they come away easily from the "core" of the fruit, which will remain on the plant once the berry has been pulled off.

Look out for
Both autumn-fruiting and golden varieties of raspberries tend to attract less bird interest compared to red summer-fruiting varieties. For protecting summer-fruiting raspberries from blackbirds, either use old CDs hanging on string from high points in the garden, which scare away birds during the fruiting period, or grow the raspberry canes in a dedicated fruit cage.

Cooking

Raspberries are one of summer's great pleasures: eager to fruit, quick to pick, and best eaten warm from the cane. Ours thrive in a quiet corner of the garden, returning year after year with their soft, blushing fruit and wild, brambly charm. While a pairing with dark chocolate is an obvious choice, why not try a touch of black pepper or a sprig of thyme? Add almond or hazelnut for warmth, or swirl them through goat's cheese for something savoury and sharp. Even a dash of aged balsamic vinegar or floral cardamom can transform them. They are a treat that invites us to think beyond the usual.

RASPBERRY CLAFOUTIS

This is a rustic French dessert with a custardy base, and tart, juicy fruit (pictured right). Clafoutis is traditionally made with cherries, but this raspberry alternative is the perfect way to enjoy a handful of any berries from your garden. It's best served warm the day it's made, but leftovers keep well in the fridge for up to 2 days and are lovely eaten when cold with a morning coffee or a spoonful of yoghurt.

Serves 4–6

Ingredients
200g (7oz) fresh raspberries

3 large eggs

80g (3oz) caster sugar

1 tsp vanilla extract or the seeds from ½ a vanilla pod

Zest of ½ an unwaxed lemon (optional)

80g (3oz) plain flour

Pinch of fine sea salt

250ml (9fl oz) whole milk

20g (¾oz) melted butter, plus extra for greasing

To serve
Icing sugar

Crème fraîche, whipped cream, or pouring cream

1. Preheat your oven to 180°C (160°C fan/350°F/Gas 4), and generously butter a round baking dish or ovenproof skillet about 20–23cm (8–9in) wide. Scatter the fresh raspberries evenly across the base and set aside.

2. In a mixing bowl, whisk the eggs and sugar together until pale and slightly frothy, then add the vanilla and lemon zest (if using). Whisk in the flour and salt until the mixture is smooth, then gradually add the milk, followed by the melted butter, whisking until the batter is thin and free of lumps. The texture should resemble single cream.

3. Let the batter rest for 10 minutes if you have time as this helps the flour to fully hydrate, which lets the custard bake more evenly.

4. Pour the batter gently over the raspberries, taking care not to dislodge them too much, then place the dish on a baking tray and bake for 30–35 minutes, or until the clafoutis is puffed, golden around the edges, and just set in the centre – it should still have a soft wobble.

5. Remove from the oven and allow to cool for 10–15 minutes. The clafoutis will naturally deflate as it cools.

6. Dust with icing sugar and serve warm or at room temperature with crème fraîche, softly whipped cream, or pouring cream.

RASPBERRY LEAF TEA

This dried herbal tea is earthy and soothing, often used to support digestion. Drink hot or chilled. Try steeping it in warm milk or cream for a subtly floral crème pâtissière, infusing it into a panna cotta or posset for a gentle, green-tea-like depth, or reducing a strong brew with honey and lemon zest into a fragrant syrup.

Harvest young, healthy leaves in late spring or early summer. Rinse and pat dry. Spread in a single layer on a clean tray or drying rack in a warm, well-ventilated space out of direct sunlight. Leave for 5–7 days, turning from time to time, until crisp. Or use a dehydrator at 40–45°C (104–113°F) for 4–6 hours. Store in an airtight jar away from light. To brew, steep 1–2 teaspoons of crumbled, dried leaves in hot water (90–95°C/194–203°F) for 5–10 minutes.

Blackberry

Key growing information

- Late winter to early spring
- 3m (10ft) between plants
- Harvest midsummer to mid-autumn
- Full sun and partial shade
- Hardy
- Medium water needs
- Medium fertility needs
- 1 plant every 3m (10ft) along a boundary
- 1.5kg (3lb 3oz) per metre of boundary

Recommended varieties

'Karaka Black', 'Loch Maree', 'Bedford Giant', 'Coolaris Patio Black', bramble (pictured right)

Growing

If you have a fence or a wall in your garden that enjoys at least a few hours of sun a day, then this is a perfect opportunity for growing blackberries in either the ground or large containers. Blackberries are trailing berries, and so they need to be tied to a vertical structure such as a fence to maximize productivity and for ease of management and harvesting.

PLANTING

The best time to plant is in late winter to early spring. Dig a hole around 45 x 45cm (18 x 18in) and mix in 2 or 3 generous spadefuls of well-rotted manure or compost. **Plant** the blackberry with around 5cm (2in) of stem depth in the ground. Firm the soil around the roots and **water** thoroughly. **Tie** any stems to the wall or fence to help the plant get underway.

MULCHING AND FEEDING

Mulch around the base of the blackberry every spring and autumn with a 7cm (3in) layer of grass, leaves, well-rotted manure, or similar. The plant sends up multiple shoots, so mulch generously around these to reduce grass growing and ensure the stems are kept clear. Liquid feed is optional, but if you wish to give the plant a boost, **feed** it when it's in flower.

PRUNING

Blackberries fruit on the previous year's growth. From the second winter after planting you need to carefully **cut out** last year's growth. Old stems have a rigid, woody texture, while new growth is smoother and very flexible. Cut the older stems to about 5cm (2in) above ground level, taking care not to damage the new stems. Remove any weak stems. Tie the strong new growth to a support system

Blackberry

such as horizontal wires on a wall or fence, leaving 25cm (10in) between each stem for maximum air flow and light, plus ease of harvesting. This will naturally create an arched or fan shape.

CONTAINER GROWING

Plant 1 dwarf blackberry such as 'Coolaris Patio Black' per container, aiming for a container at least 50cm (20in) in diameter for the best results. Container-grown blackberries will benefit from a liquid feed every 4 weeks during spring and summer.

HARVEST

When fruits have turned their distinctively black colour they can be gently picked off. If there is any resistance they aren't quite ready for harvest. Pick ripe fruits regularly to beat the birds.

Alternative crops

There are many other types of trailing berries you can grow in the same way, such as tayberries, loganberries, sylvanberries, and even Japanese wineberries. Most excitingly, each berry type has its own distinct look and flavour.

Look out for

Use CDs to create visual deterrents for blackbirds (see p.175).

Cooking

BLACKBERRY GIN

There's something deeply satisfying about capturing the last of summer in a bottle. Blackberry gin is rich, dark, and gently sweet, like hedgerow jam with a kick. The berries lend an inky hue and a deep, juicy warmth, balanced by the botanicals of the gin and a whisper of citrus or spice if you choose. It's the sort of thing best made with purple-stained fingers on a rainy afternoon and stored away for colder nights. It keeps well in a sealed bottle in a cool, dark place for up to a year. The flavour mellows and matures over time.

Makes approximately 700ml (25fl oz)

Ingredients

500g (1lb 2oz) ripe blackberries (fresh or frozen)

250g (9oz) caster sugar

700ml (25fl oz) gin (a decent mid-range London Dry works well)

Strip of zest from an unwaxed lemon or orange, a cinnamon stick, or a few bruised juniper berries (optional)

Equipment

Large glass jar or bottle (at least 1 litre/1¾ pints capacity), sterilized (see p.28)

750ml (1¼ pint) glass bottle, sterilized (see p.28)

1. Wash the blackberries and gently pat them dry. If using frozen berries, let them thaw first as they'll break down more easily and release their juice faster.

2. Tip the blackberries into the large jar along with the sugar. Add any optional aromatics if desired – a strip of citrus peel adds brightness, a cinnamon stick adds warmth, and juniper offers sharp, dry, slightly medicinal notes. Pour over the gin, seal tightly, and give it a good shake to dissolve the sugar.

3. Place the jar in a cool, dark place and shake it every day for the first week. The sugar will fully dissolve, and the berries will begin to infuse the spirit with colour and flavour. Allow the gin to steep for 4 weeks, or longer if you prefer a deeper, more syrupy result.

4. Once the infusion is to your liking, strain through a fine mesh sieve or muslin into a smaller, sterilized bottle, pressing gently on the berries to extract all the juice. Store out of direct sunlight to preserve the colour. Discard the solids or save them for baking into boozy crumbles or brownies.

Alternative recipes

Swap some of the sugar for honey for a more herbal, mellow sweetness. For a garden twist, add a few thyme sprigs. For more variation, try with sloes, damsons, or elderberries.

Ways to serve …

There are lots of ways to use your blackberry gin:

On ice Serve neat or top with tonic or sparkling water, or mix it into cocktails.

Bramble cocktail Mix with lemon juice, syrup, and crème de mûre.

Autumnal spritz Swirl a spoonful into Prosecco.

Blackberry

Blueberry

Key growing information

- Late autumn or late winter
- 1m (3ft) between plants
- Harvest mid- to late summer
- Full sun
- Hardy
- Medium water needs
- Medium fertility needs
- 1 plant per sq m
- 3kg (6½lb) per sq m

Recommended varieties

'Bluecrop' (pictured right), 'Chandler'

Growing

When grown in the right conditions, blueberries provide generous crops of pure deliciousness! They need acidic soil to grow strongly; if your soil is not acidic, their growth will be weak or non-existent, but you can grow them in containers (see opposite). Many varieties need to be grown with pollination partners (a different variety that flowers at the same time) for maximum yields. The 2 varieties we've shared here do well if you grow 2 or 3 plants of the same type as they are better at self pollinating but, for the absolute best results, grow a couple of both varieties.

PLANTING

Make a planting hole 45 x 45cm (18 x 18in) and mix around 200g (7oz) of sulphur powder with the soil, plus a couple of large spadefuls of compost or well-rotted manure. **Plant** at the depth at which the plant was growing in its container (visible as a colour change on the stem just above the roots), firm, and **water** well.

MULCHING AND FEEDING

Mulch blueberries with organic material such as woodchip or leaves to keep the area free from grass and to maintain soil moisture. **Feed** the plant every 3

weeks during flowering and fruiting (see p.13).

PRUNING

For the first 2 years lightly **prune** blueberries in late winter, focusing on shape, and removing any odd or weak growth. Then, again in late winter, remove the oldest (thickest) 1 or 2 stems every year by cutting to the base of the plant to encourage more shoots, and make sure each main stem has space to breathe. Cut out any branches growing inwards to encourage a clear centre. Aim to maintain a mix of different-aged stems (say 6 or 7 stems that are 1–4 years old). This range helps with consistent fruiting.

CONTAINER GROWING

Blueberries do very well in large containers of at least 45cm (18in) diameter. Fill with a 50:50 mix of topsoil and compost, with 200g (7oz) of sulphur powder mixed in, and **plant** to the same depth it was in its pot. **Mulch** with 5cm (2in) of peat-free ericaceous compost every spring thereafter. Water well during fruit formation.

HARVEST

Harvest fruits when they are fully blue, with no hints of red or green on the flesh, and have a dusty bloom that you can wipe away with a finger. When ripe, the berries will come off the plant easily when picked.

Alternative crop

Honeyberries are elongated blueberry-like fruits that grow in a very similar way to blueberries but do not need acidic soil to thrive, making them ideal to plant directly in the ground. Make sure you plant two varieties that will cross pollinate for the best yields.

Look out for

Blackbirds may eat the fruits (see p.172).

Cooking

🫙 BLUEBERRY COULIS

Smooth like liquid velvet, sweet with a restrained tang, never as sharp as raspberries or as sugary as strawberries, blueberry coulis is a thin purée with hints of wine, forest, and hedgerows. When made well, it tastes like the scent of crushed blueberries warmed in the sun: rich, slightly floral, and just tart enough to keep you coming back for another spoonful. Use over pancakes, yoghurt, and ice cream, or to finish a perfect cheesecake (see opposite).

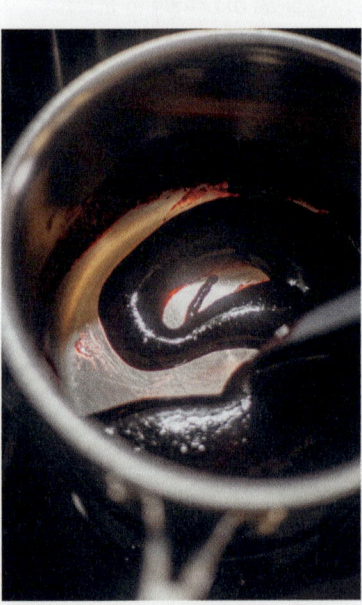

Makes 1 x 250ml (9fl oz) bottle

Ingredients

250g (9oz) fresh or frozen blueberries

2 tbsp caster sugar (adjust to taste)

1 tsp lemon juice

1. Place the blueberries, sugar, and lemon juice in a small saucepan over a medium heat. Stir gently until the berries begin to release their juice. Simmer the mixture for 5–8 minutes, stirring often, until the berries are soft and the liquid slightly syrupy.

2. Blend the mixture using a hand-held blender or food processor until smooth. For a refined texture, press through a fine sieve to remove the skins. If the mixture is too thick, loosen with a spoonful of water (pictured left).

3. Let it cool completely, then store it in the fridge for up to a week, or freeze in small portions for 6–9 months.

🔪 CHEESECAKE WITH BLUEBERRY COULIS

This creamy vanilla cheesecake is everything you want it to be: smooth, lightly tangy, and perfectly balanced. Crowned with rich blueberry coulis swirled into soft ribbons, it's as elegant as it is indulgent, a quiet showstopper that tastes like late summer and feels like the reward you deserve after a long day in the garden. Allow plenty of time (at least 5 hours) for the cheesecake to cool and chill after baking and before you serve it.

Serves 8–10

Ingredients
For the crust

200g (7oz) digestive or plain biscuits

100g (3½oz) unsalted butter, melted

For the filling

500g (1lb 2oz) full-fat cream cheese at room temperature

100g (3½oz) caster sugar

1 tbsp plain flour

1 tsp vanilla extract

Zest of 1 unwaxed lemon

3 large eggs, room temperature

150ml (5fl oz) sour cream

100ml (3½fl oz) blueberry coulis (prepared ahead, see opposite)

To finish
Icing sugar

1. Preheat the oven to 160°C (140°C fan/325°F/Gas 3). Line the base of a 20cm (8in) springform tin with baking parchment.

2. Blitz the biscuits into fine crumbs, stir in the melted butter, then press it firmly into the base of the tin and slightly up the sides. Bake for 10 minutes, then let it cool.

3. Beat the cream cheese, sugar, flour, vanilla extract, and lemon zest until the mixture is utterly smooth. Beat in the eggs one at a time, then the sour cream, and mix enough to combine.

4. Pour the filling into the tin on top of the cooled crust, then drop spoonfuls of blueberry coulis across the surface; use a thin skewer to swirl it in spirals.

5. Bake for 45–50 minutes until the edges are set and the centre wobbles softly. Switch off the oven, open the door slightly, and leave to cool for an hour to prevent cracking.

6. Chill in the fridge for at least 4 hours, or overnight. Sprinkle with a little icing sugar to serve.

Gooseberry

Key growing information

- Late autumn or late winter
- 1m (3ft) between plants
- Harvest early summer
- Full sun
- Hardy
- Medium water needs
- Low fertility needs
- 1 plant per sq m
- 3–5kg (6½–11lb) per sq m

Recommended varieties
'Invicta' (pictured opposite below), 'Hinnonmaki Red', 'Hinnonmaki Yellow'

Growing

Gooseberries are one of the most productive fruits you can grow! Most commonly known for being green and a little sharp, they also come in very sweet yellow and red varieties.

PLANTING

Add 2 generous spadefuls of well-rotted manure or compost to a 30 x 30cm (12 x 12in) planting hole, and **plant** the bush at the same depth it was previously planted – you can see this on the stem where the shade of the bark changes just above the roots. Firm the soil around the stem and roots then **water** well.

MULCHING AND FEEDING

Mulch your gooseberries in late winter or early spring with a 7cm (3in) layer of organic material such as woodchips or straw. Leave a 5cm (2in) gap clear of mulch around the main stem of the gooseberry. They do not need to be fed.

PRUNING

In summer, after fruiting, and once new growth has about 8 leaves, **cut it back** to 5 leaves to encourage more fruiting points the following year. Then do the main pruning in winter by removing any dead, weak, or crossing growth to maintain good air flow. Focus on keeping stems that show strong outward growth, and cut their side branches back to 3 buds to maintain form and vigour.

CONTAINER GROWING

Plant 1 gooseberry per standard container then **prune** it so there are 3 or 4 main stems as a way of limiting the plant to suit the container size. **Feed** with a liquid feed every 4 weeks over spring and summer. In later years, follow the pruning advice for plants in the ground.

HARVEST
When gooseberries have a little give when squeezed, similar to a grape, they are ready to be harvested. Carefully pull the fruits away from the plant, taking care to avoid the spikes on the stems.

Alternative crop
Though not a gooseberry, the cape gooseberry (pictured right) is a tender plant that can be grown from seed in a polytunnel or a sunny, sheltered spot as an annual. It produces lantern-like husks that turn brown as they mature and are crispy to touch. If you remove the husks you reveal a delicious small, orange fruit inside. They are very easy to grow and have almost no pest or disease issues.

Look out for
Gooseberry sawfly caterpillars can strip plants of all leaves in a matter of days. They are most prominent around mid-spring to early summer. Keep an eye on your gooseberries, and if you see any damage then pick off the caterpillars, returning daily until there is no further damage.

Cooking

Gooseberries are the tart, green jewels of early summer, their sharpness mellowing as they ripen to blush pink and gold. Long used in crumbles, fools, and jams, they have a bright, citrusy flavour that also cuts beautifully through oily fish or rich roast pork. For me, their sharp–sweet taste is a reminder of childhood gardens and the first harvest of the season.

GOOSEBERRY CURD

There's a peculiar beauty to gooseberries. Slightly awkward, green or blushed and veined like marbles, they rarely demand the spotlight, but simmer them down and they soften into something floral, sharp, and entirely their own.

This gooseberry curd is less loud than lemon curd, more complex on the tongue, and perfect for preserving a glut from the garden. It's sharp and sweet, softly set, and a joy to spoon. Use it in tarts, on warm pancakes, spread thick on toast with cold butter, stirred into yoghurt, or spread under a layer of strawberries in a tart. It's also glorious with scones.

Makes 2–3 small jars

Ingredients
300g (10oz) gooseberries, rinsed, topped, and tailed

Elderflower blossom (optional)

Juice of 1 lemon

100g (3½oz) unsalted butter, cubed

250g (9oz) granulated sugar

3 large eggs, beaten and strained

Equipment
Jam thermometer (optional)

3 x 400ml (14fl oz) jars, sterilized (see p.28)

1. Add the gooseberries (and optional elderflower blossom) to a saucepan with the lemon juice and a splash of water (pictured top right). Warm gently, stirring now and then, until the fruit splits (about 10–20 minutes). Push the pulp through a sieve into a bowl to remove skins and seeds, leaving a smooth, tart purée.

2. Measure out 200ml (7fl oz) of purée and add it to a heatproof bowl with the butter and sugar (pictured bottom right). Place the bowl

over a pan of simmering water (don't let the base touch the water). Stir until the butter melts and the sugar dissolves fully.

3. Remove the bowl from the pan to let the mixture cool a

little so it is warm enough to cook the egg, but not so hot that it risks scrambling. Stir in the strained eggs slowly, whisking constantly.

4. Replace the bowl over the simmering pan and stir patiently for 10–15 minutes, until the curd thickens enough to coat the back of a spoon. If using a jam thermometer, it should reach about 82°C (180°F).

5. Pour into warm, sterilized jars and seal immediately. Once cool, refrigerate. It keeps for 3–4 weeks unopened in the fridge; use within a week once opened.

Blackcurrant

Key growing information

- Late autumn or late winter
- 1m (3ft) between plants
- Harvest mid- to late summer
- Full sun
- Hardy
- Medium water needs
- Medium fertility needs
- 1 plant per sq m
- 4–5kg (8¾–11lb) per sq m

Recommended varieties

'Ben Connan', 'Ben Hope' (pictured right and far right), 'Big Ben', 'Ben Sarek'

Growing

Blackcurrants are an excellent fruit for any garden as they're easy to grow, offering high yields, and are somewhat less favoured by blackbirds than other berries thanks to their colour. The small, black, glossy fruits look like dark pearls in the rain, and pack a punch when it comes to flavour.

PLANTING

Dig a hole 45 x 45cm (18 x 18in) and mix in 3 generous spadefuls of well-rotted manure or compost. Then, **plant** the blackcurrant plant 10cm (4in) deeper than it was previously planted. Firm the soil around the roots and **water** thoroughly. The deep planting will encourage it to send up more shoots – blackcurrants do best as more of a collection of stems emerging from the ground than as a single-stemmed plant with branches.

MULCHING AND FEEDING

Keep blackcurrants clear of weeds at all times, and **mulch** around the base with grass clippings, woodchip, or other similar materials. Blackcurrants also respond well to a mulch of compost in early spring ahead of the new season; this will add nutrients as well as suppressing weeds. There is no need for additional feed.

PRUNING

Don't prune in the first winter. Every winter afterwards **prune** out any dead or weak growth, and remove one-third of the oldest stems (those that are thickest at the base), cutting them back to ground level. Aim to have equal spacing between each stem, and a mix of stems aged between 1 and 3 years old.

Blackcurrant

CONTAINER GROWING
Plant 1 compact variety of blackcurrant, such as 'Ben Sarek', per standard container at the same depth as if you were planting in the ground (see Planting). **Mulch** well with a 5cm (2in) layer of leaves or grass clippings, ensuring there is a layer of mulch at all times, and **feed** in mid-spring and again in early summer (see p.13).

HARVEST
Blackcurrants are best harvested a few days after they have turned fully black. They are ready when you give them a squeeze and they have a little give – they feel rock hard when unripe. Pull individual berries or whole trusses of fruit away from the plant.

Look out for
Blackbirds may eat the fruits (see p.172).

Cooking

Blackcurrants are sharp, rich, and unmistakably bold, the kind of fruit that demands attention. Traditionally turned into cordials, jams, or folded through summer puddings, their deep flavour works just as well in pies and fools as it does in savoury sauces for game or lamb. There's something nostalgic about their dark, staining juice, a quintessential flavour of hedgerows and of homemade preserves.

BLACKCURRANT BOSHI

I thought I'd introduce you to a different offering, one that is salty, sour, and deeply satisfying: salted, fermented blackcurrants, based on the Japanese technique for *umeboshi* (salted Japanese plum). This version amplifies the incredible richness of blackcurrants and turns them into a fragrant pairing for savoury meals with no more than salt and time.

Makes 1 small jar

Ingredients
200g (7oz) fresh blackcurrants, stems removed

20–25g (¾–1oz) sea salt (10–12% of the fruit's weight)

Equipment
1 x 200g (7oz) jar, sterilized (see p.28)

1. Rinse your blackcurrants gently and remove any leaves or damaged berries. Pat them dry, then weigh them. Calculate 10–12% of that weight in sea salt.

2. In a clean, sterilized jar, layer the berries with the salt. Press down lightly with a clean spoon to bruise the berries and help them release juice. You want them to begin steeping in their own brine.

3. Cover the container with a lid and let it sit at room temperature (18–22°C/64–72°F) out of direct sunlight. Over the next few days, the salt will draw out more juice, forming a deep purple brine. Stir daily and press down to keep the fruit submerged. If needed, add a clean weight or a small jar to hold the fruit under the brine.

4. Let the berries ferment for 1 month. Taste them: they should be tart, salty, and slightly funky. If they smell yeasty or foul, don't eat them. Once they reach the flavour you like, transfer them to a sterilized jar and refrigerate. The flavour will deepen over time.

Alternative recipe
For a more traditional *boshi* texture, strain the fermented berries, reserving the brine, and lay them out on a rack

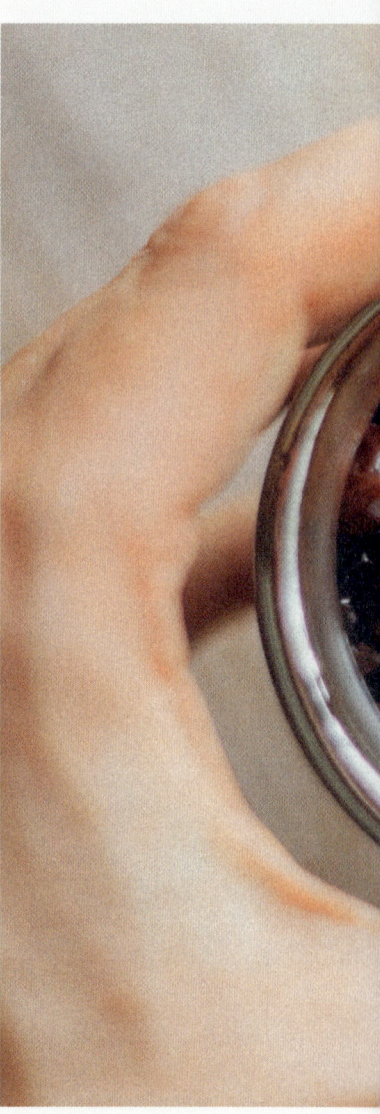

Blackcurrant

or parchment-lined tray. Sun dry for 2 days, or until leathery and pliable, then store in a jar with a dash of their brine in the fridge for up to a year (they continue to improve with time).

Meals with …

Use your blackcurrant **boshi** *to brighten dishes.*

With rice or grain bowls Add a few berries for a tangy punch.

Inside *onigiri* **(rice balls)** Tuck a single blackcurrant *boshi* into the centre of a rice ball. Its salty–sour punch balances the mild rice beautifully.

With steamed rice Serve one or two berries on a bowl of plain rice. The brine and fruit offer a vibrant contrast, cleansing the palate and sharpening the appetite.

In *ochazuke* **(tea-poured rice)** Place a berry in a bowl of cooked rice, then pour over hot green tea or light *dashi* broth. It adds a fruity acidity and savoury edge to this comforting dish.

As a pickled side Include a few blackcurrant *boshi* in a bento box as a tart–savoury element to cut through richer or fried foods.

In clear broths or soups Drop one *boshi* into a mild soup or miso broth for a subtle infusion of sourness and umami.

Redcurrant

Key growing information

- ⚓ Late autumn or late winter
- ↔ 1m (3ft) between plants
- 📅 Harvest mid- to late summer
- ☀ Full sun
- ❄ Hardy
- 💧 Medium water needs
- Medium fertility needs
- 1 plant per sq m
- 3–4kg (6½–9lb) per sq m

Recommended varieties

'Rovada', 'Jonkheer Van Tets'

Growing

Sweet, juicy, and delicious, redcurrants have an almost glow-in-the dark feel about them with their translucent red berries.

PLANTING
Dig a hole 45 x 45cm (18 x 18in) and mix in 3 generous spadefuls of well-rotted manure or compost. **Plant** your redcurrant at the same depth as it was growing previously. Firm the soil around the roots, and **water** well.

MULCHING
Mulch with a 5cm (2in) layer of grass clippings, woodchip, or well-rotted manure, but leave 5cm (2in) clear around the stem. There is no need to feed.

PRUNING
In winter, **cut back** all new growth by one-third to just above an outward-facing bud to encourage a goblet-shaped bush. This also means pruning any branches growing into the centre of the plant so it remains clear. Aim for the bush to have between 5 and 7 core branches to create the goblet shape, and remove any weak growth.

CONTAINER GROWING
Plant a redcurrant in a standard container, but when **pruning** select only 3 core branches to make the goblet shape described above. **Mulch** generously with a 5cm (2in) layer of organic material such as grass clippings, and **feed** in mid-spring and early summer.

HARVEST
Harvest the fruit when all the currants on an entire truss (a string of currants coming off the plant) are fully red in colour.

Look out for
Blackbirds will try to eat the redcurrants. As well as following the advice for blackberries (see p.179), redcurrants are best protected by purchasing a fruit bush net or cover where you remove the whole cover to harvest the ripe fruits.

Cooking

REDCURRANT JELLY

There are few preserves more beautiful than redcurrant jelly. Jewel-bright and translucent when spread, and rich and dark in a jar, it captures the sharp thrill of summer's red fruit in its purest, most elegant form. Unlike jam, it's silky and seedless, made to be spooned onto lamb chops, stirred into gravies, melted into glazes, or served with sharp cheese and crusty bread. The jelly keeps for a year unopened in a cool, dark place. Use to transform roasts, cheeses, sauces, and even cocktails with a gleaming burst of brilliance.

Makes 2–3 small jars (about 400ml/14fl oz in total)

Ingredients
500g (1lb 2oz) fresh redcurrants, stems on

400g (14oz) granulated sugar (per 500ml/16fl oz juice extracted)

Equipment
Small jars, sterilized (see p.28)

Jelly bag or muslin-lined sieve

1. Rinse the redcurrants gently, then simmer with 100ml (3½fl oz) water for 10–15 minutes until the fruits have collapsed. Strain through a jelly bag or muslin-lined sieve overnight. Don't be tempted to press them, or the jelly won't be clear.

2. The next day, measure the juice and return to heat in the pan. For every 500ml (16fl oz) of juice, add 400g (14oz) sugar. Stir to dissolve the sugar, then boil hard until it reaches 104–105°C (219–221°F) or a small spoonful on a chilled plate wrinkles when pressed.

3. Skim off any foam and pour into the sterilized jars. Seal immediately.

Tip
This recipe only works with fresh redcurrants. When the currants are frozen, the pectin in the redcurrants, which is needed to set the jelly, breaks down.

Rhubarb

Key growing information

- Late autumn or late winter
- 60cm (24in) between plants
- Harvest early spring to midsummer
- Full sun
- Hardy
- High water needs
- High fertility needs
- 2 plants per sq m
- 7–8kg (15½–18lb) per sq m

Recommended varieties

'Timperley Early', 'Champagne', 'Victoria' (pictured right)

Growing

If only everything was as productive as rhubarb! Its beautiful stems emerge from a "crown" just under the ground from early spring, and offer continuous harvests until midsummer.

PLANTING

Rhubarb comes in pots or as bare root crowns consisting of roots and at least 1 bud. Create a large hole the width and depth of two spade heads, and add 4 or 5 generous spades of well-rotted manure or compost. **Plant** crowns in winter 5cm (2in) below ground level, while potted rhubarb can be planted at the same level as in the pot. Firm in, and **water** well.

MULCHING AND FEEDING

Rhubarb is a very hungry crop so **mulch** in late winter with a 5–7cm (2–3in) layer of well-rotted manure or compost. Liquid **feed** on a monthly basis through spring and summer. **Water** well during harvest season if it hasn't rained for a week to maintain good stem production.

DIVIDING

Each autumn allow the plant to naturally die back. Every 4 or 5 years lift the crown and use a sharp spade to **split** it into 3 or 4 sections, each with at least 1 bud, then replant. Dividing the crown maintains plant vigour.

CONTAINER GROWING

Rhubarb is only suitable for larger containers at least 50cm (20in) in diameter. **Mulch** with leaves or grass clippings to retain moisture, and liquid **feed** every 3 weeks in spring and summer.

HARVEST

Avoid harvesting in the first year to allow the plant to mature. Then, harvest no more than one-third of the stems at a time, stopping around midsummer. Grab the base of a chosen stem and firmly pull in an up-and-outward motion. Remove the leaf as this cannot be eaten.

Look out for

Slugs cause damage (p.107).

Cooking

RHUBARB IN THE KITCHEN
Rhubarb is one of the great shape-shifters of the garden, both a fruit and not a fruit, tart as lemon but with a blush like rose petals. While it's most often stewed with sugar or tucked into crumbles, its uses stretch far beyond puddings.

Roasted rhubarb
Try roasting thick batons with orange zest and a touch of honey until tender, then serving them with yoghurt or grilled meats.

In chutney
Add diced rhubarb to chutneys or barbecue sauces for sharpness and structure.

Rhubarb juice
One of rhubarb's most overlooked gifts is its juice. Simmer chopped stalks with a splash of water, then strain through a muslin cloth. The result is a vivid pink liquid, tart and bright, with a perfume that citrus can't match. Use this juice anywhere you'd reach for lemon: whisked into vinaigrettes, drizzled over grilled fish, stirred into sorbets, or brightening a sweet glaze. It's a brilliant local stand-in for imported acidity during the early summer months. Freeze rhubarb juice in ice cube trays for year-round zing.

Edible Flowers

Why Grow Flowers Too?

Traditionally, flowers have been seen as a waste of valuable space in kitchen gardens, but they have become far more prominent in the modern kitchen garden and allotment because they have proven themselves to offer multiple benefits for both the garden and gardener. Here are our four favourite reasons to grow flowers alongside crops.

EDIBLE

Firstly, many flowers are edible and can be enjoyed at the dinner table, offering wonderful pops of colour to garnish not only meals, but drinks, too. As well as the flowers featured in this chapter, many vegetables and herbs, such as runner beans, courgettes, thyme, and chives, provide edible flowers, too.

The range of uses that edible flowers contribute to the kitchen may seem limited to garnishes in salads and drinks, but their flavours and aromas can vary hugely.

Borage offers a refreshing cucumber-like infusion to chilled water, while calendula (pot marigold) petals boast a peppery bitterness that complements soups, salads, eggs, and rice. Flowering herbs have heavily fragranced petals that range from perfumed thyme, oregano, and rosemary, to the moreish allium kick of chives, all of which are perfect to infuse and flavour vinegars. Lesser-known edibles such as runner bean flowers provide a pretty pop of colour and unique sweet, beany flavour with which to garnish dishes.

VISUAL

It goes without saying that flowers are beautiful to look at. Having colour among the calming green of the garden creates much joy, and the more beautiful your garden is, the more time you'll want to spend there and tend it. This supports the old proverb which says that the best fertilizer is the gardener's shadow.

Growing flowers among your vegetables has many benefits as well as being visually pleasing; for more information, see polyculture, page 18.

BENEFICIAL

Think of flowers as recruitment officers, bringing in as many beneficial insects as possible, such as hoverflies, lacewings, and bumblebees, to your garden to help create a balanced ecosystem, with healthy, productive crops. Growing a few flowers will really help!

We also think that many non-edible flowers, such as poppies, *Cosmos bipinnatus*, nigella, foxgloves (though loved by pollinators, foxgloves are highly poisonous to people), and rudbeckia, are worth growing in an edible garden simply because of how effective they are at encouraging insects.

DECORATIONAL

As well as enjoying flowers in the garden and on your plate, you can create your own bouquets. The industrial flower industry is very damaging to the environment, so growing your own flowers to put in vases around the house (and gift to friends) has many more benefits than you might have initially considered.

Two simple rules of thumb for choosing flowers for arranging is to have a thriller (such as rose), a filler (such as zinnia), and a spiller (such as nasturtium) – and to work with odd numbers of stems. The rest is down to your personal preference!

Nasturtium

Key growing information

- Mid-spring to midsummer
- 1cm (½in) sowing depth
- 45cm (18in) between clumps of plants
- 8 weeks to harvest
- Full sun
- Tender
- Medium water needs
- High fertility needs
- 3 (clumps) per sq m
- 0.5–1kg (1–2¼lb) per sq m, leaves and flowers

Recommended varieties

'Climbing Mixed' (pictured near right), 'Tip-Top Apricot'; Canary creeper (climbing nasturtium species)

Growing

This is a spicy-tasting, fast-growing plant, all of which (including the flower) is edible. It's perfect for filling spaces as it will sprawl across the ground and down the edges of beds and pots.

STAGE 1

Fill a 9cm (3½in) pot with compost. Make a shallow bowl indentation in the centre and **sow** 4 or 5 seeds, then gently cover with compost. **Water** well.

STAGE 2

Once seedlings have appeared, **thin** to the 3 strongest (if all have germinated) and allow them to continue growing until they reach around 15cm (6in) tall, ready to plant out.

STAGE 3

Use a trowel to make a hole the size of the pot, then gently remove the rootball from the pot and **transplant** the clump into the hole. Firm it in using your fingers, and water thoroughly.

CONTAINER GROWING

Plant 1 potted clump of plants (stage 3) per container.

HARVEST

Start to harvest nasturtium leaves once the plant is at least 30 x 30cm (12 x 12in) in size. Pick flowers as and when needed, but consider leaving a few for the bees to enjoy. These will turn into green, unripe seeds, which can be pickled as a caper alternative (see opposite).

Look out for

Pick off any cabbage white caterpillars and squash any yellow eggs you see on the leaves. Nasturtium is often planted as a companion plant to draw cabbage white butterflies away from your brassicas.

Nasturtium

Cooking

NASTURTIUMS IN THE KITCHEN
Bright, spicy nasturtiums are among the most giving plants in the garden, and are also entirely edible from leaf to seed. Their peppery heat, somewhere between rocket and wasabi, can be preserved and enjoyed in three distinct, delicious ways.

Leaves
Their leaves, especially young ones, blend beautifully into pesto. Pulse with olive oil, garlic, toasted nuts, and hard cheese or nutritional yeast for a punchy, verdant paste, perfect with roasted vegetables, warm new potatoes, or slathered inside a sandwich.

Flowers
Vibrant and fiery, the flowers make a stunning infused vinegar. Loosely fill a clean jar with petals, top with mild white wine or apple cider vinegar, and steep for a week or two, shaking the jar each day to avoid spoilage. Strain and bottle. It becomes a peppery pink-red elixir for dressings, marinades, or deglazing pans.

Nasturtium capers
Harvest the green, unripe seeds while they are still plump. Rinse, then drain, and pack into warmed sterilized jars. Cover with hot white wine vinegar, infused with mustard seeds or bay leaf if you like, and a little sugar or honey to taste, and a pinch of salt, then seal. After 2–3 weeks, they become sharp little flavour bombs, brilliant scattered over eggs, cured fish, or salads. They make a great, mildly spicy olive alternative.

Edible Flowers

Rose

Key growing information

- Climbing roses, 2m (6½ft) between plants
- Rambling roses, 6m (20ft) between plants
- Shrub roses, 1m (3ft) between plants
- Harvest flowers mid-spring to early summer, hips late summer to mid-autumn
- Full sun and partial shade
- Hardy
- Medium water needs
- Medium fertility needs

Recommended varieties

Climbing 'The Generous Gardener' (pictured top right, pale pink, scented blooms); **Rambling** 'Paul's Himalayan Musk' (most gorgeous visual display of pastel pink puffs of blooms); **Shrub** *Rosa rugosa* (pictured below right, perfect for large hips)

Growing

Roses are arguably the most loved flower worldwide. The best one to start with is *Rosa rugosa*. A wild rose, its wonderful scented blooms turn into large hips, making it ideal for culinary use. It is also very hardy and disease resistant.

STAGE 1

Aim to plant in early to mid-spring. Make a hole larger than the roots of the rose plant, whether it's potted or bare root (many roses are sold in winter without soil around their roots). Add 2 generous spadefuls of compost or well-rotted manure at the base and mix this with some soil. **Plant** your rose so the graft union (the swollen area where the rose variety is grafted onto the rootstock) is 5cm (2in) below ground level. Fill the hole and **water** well.

STAGE 2

Mulch the rose with compost, well-rotted manure, or woodchip, spreading it to a radius of at least 45cm (18in), with a gap around the stem for good air flow.

STAGE 3

At the end of the first season, cut back all growth to 30cm (12in) above the ground, then reapply the mulch. **Mulch** annually in late winter.

PRUNING

For all roses, remove any dead, weak, or damaged growth in winter, and prune shrub roses by one-third.

Cooking

ROSES IN THE KITCHEN

Bringing more than beauty, roses also carry a bold, aromatic flavour that's equally at home in sweet and savoury dishes. Their scent is layered: honeyed, slightly citrusy, with hints of sherbet, tea, even musk, and often with a whisper of spice. Used well, roses can transform the ordinary into something beautiful.

Rose-infused gin
This is a simple starting point. Add freshly picked petals or hips (about a handful) to 500ml (16fl oz) of good gin. Let it steep for 2–3 weeks, then strain. The result is a pale-coloured spirit with floral top notes, perfect for cocktails with citrus or cucumber.

Rose syrup
Gently stir and simmer petals with equal parts sugar and water (enough to cover the petals), for 10–15 minutes. Strain, cool, and add a squeeze of lemon juice to preserve the colour and flavour, then bottle and store in a fridge for up to 4 weeks. Use it in iced teas, cakes, or to glaze fruit. For savoury use, try adding a few drops of rose syrup to dressings or with lamb and spicy dishes.

Rose salt
Blitz 2 parts rose petals with 3 parts flaky sea salt, then dry them spread out thinly over a clean tea towel by an open window until crisp. Subtle and fragrant, this is wonderful on shortbread, roasted roots, or sprinkled over feta.

Rose hips
Rich in vitamin C, rose hips make stunning jams or jellies (see p.173 and p.195, and substitute rose hips for the fruits). Always remove the seeds and irritating hairs inside the hips before eating; this is most easily done by passing the cooked jams, jellies, or syrups through a fine mesh strainer such as a jelly bag.

CONTAINER GROWING
Plant a rose in a dedicated container at least 45 litres (12 gallons) in volume.

HARVEST
Use snips or secateurs to cut flowers (or hips) where the base of the flower (or hip) meets the stem.

Look out for
Aphids may cluster on the tips of your rose plants. If you see them, blast them off with a strong jet of water.

More Flowers

Edible flowers are easy to grow, add so much joy to a garden, and provide vital food for pollinators and other beneficial insects. Many add another dimension to your meals and drinks, too. Here are some great annual edible flowers that we think every garden should have.

SULPHUR COSMOS

- Mid-spring to midsummer
- 1cm (½in) sowing depth
- 25cm (10cm) between plants
- 12 weeks to first flowers
- Full sun
- Half hardy
- Medium water needs
- Medium fertility needs

Recommended varieties

'Cosmic Red', 'Cosmic Orange', 'Limara Lemon'

Popular with natural dyers, sulphur cosmos (*Cosmos sulphureus*, pictured below) also provides edible blooms which certainly aren't shy with their vivid colours. Some varieties grow up to 1.2m (4ft) tall, making them even harder to miss. **Sow** 2 seeds into a 7cm (3in) pot, **thin** to the strongest, and **plant out** once 4 or 5 true leaves have appeared. **In the kitchen** it's rather bitter to taste, so use as a light garnish.

CALENDULA

- Mid-spring to midsummer
- 1cm (½in) sowing depth
- 30cm (12in) between plants
- 8 weeks to first flowers
- Full sun
- Hardy
- Medium water needs
- Medium fertility needs

Recommended varieties

'Art Shades Mix', 'Canteloupe'

Calendula (pot marigold, pictured above right) is a joyful and hardworking plant with edible leaves and flowers. It's a popular companion plant due to its attractiveness to beneficial insects, and resilience. The species itself is a great addition, as well as its many varieties. It readily self seeds, so leave a couple of plants to flower and seed for free plants next year which you can move about the garden. **Sow** seeds directly, or sow 2 seeds per 7cm (3in) pot, **thin** to the strongest, and **plant out** once 4 or 5 true leaves have appeared. **In the kitchen** use a few petals to add a pop of colour to dishes.

More Flowers

ZINNIA

- Mid-spring to early summer
- 0.5cm (¼in) sowing depth
- 30cm (12in) between plants
- 12 weeks to first flowers
- Full sun
- Half hardy
- Low water needs
- Medium fertility needs

Recommended varieties

'Queen Lime Mix', 'Lilliput White', 'Oklahoma Salmon'

Zinnias (pictured below) are breathtaking cut flowers, particularly the 'Queen Lime' varieties. They look wonderful among vegetables, and their petals are edible, too. They also do a great job at attracting pollinators. **Sow** 2 or 3 seeds per 7cm (3in) pot, **thin** to the strongest, and **plant out** once seedlings are 10cm (4in) tall. Slugs (see p.107) may damage them. **In the kitchen** the petals are rather bitter to taste, so use sparingly to garnish.

BORAGE

- Mid-spring to midsummer
- 1cm (½in) sowing depth
- 45cm (18in) between plants
- 8 weeks to first flowers
- Full sun
- Half hardy
- Medium water needs
- Low fertility needs

Recommended varieties

Common borage (blue), 'Alba'

These unique star-shaped flowers (pictured above) come typically in blues and whites, though you will often spot flowers on your plants with pink and purple hues, too. Borage produces a truly beautiful crop with hundreds of edible flowers per plant. Like calendula, borage readily self seeds. **Sow** 2 seeds into a 7cm (3in) pot, and thin to the strongest. **Transplant** pot-grown seedlings when 5 or 6 true leaves are present. **In the kitchen** add the flowers to chilled drinks and cold dishes like salads for a flash of colour and refreshing cucumber flavour.

Kitchen Crop Masterplan

This chart is your go-to guide for the kitchen after harvesting, detailing how to store crops if you're not ready to cook with them straight away, cooking techniques, and preserving options. Some crops, like leafy greens, are best eaten fresh, but most can be stored for weeks or even months with the right care.

	Crop	Storage	Dehydration	Freezing in portions
ROOT VEGETABLES	Potato	Cure (2 weeks), then store 1–6°C, dark, ventilated (7–8 months)	Slice, blanch (2 mins), dry 55°C (8–12 hours), avoid waxy potatoes	Turn into mash before freezing (9–12 months)
	Carrot	Cure (2–3 days), then store 0–3°C; or layer in damp sand (6 months)	Slice, blanch (3 mins), dry 50°C (6–10 hours)	Blanch (2–5 mins), roast, or steam before freezing (9–12 months)
	Parsnip	Leave in ground, protect from harsh frost or layer in damp sand (7–8 months)	Slice, blanch (2 mins), dry 55°C (10–12 hours)	Turn into mash before freezing (9–12 months)
	Swede	Store 3–5°C; or layer in damp sand (7–8 months)	Slice, blanch (4 mins), dry 60°C (6–10 hours)	Blanch (3–4 mins), portion, and freeze (6–12 months)
	Beetroot	Leave in ground, protect, use as needed; or layer in damp sand (7–8 months)	Slice thinly and dry 55°C (8–12 hours)	Boil whole (25–35 mins), roast, or steam before freezing (9–12 months)
	Radish	Leave in ground, protect, use as needed	Slice thinly and dry 52°C (7–12 hours)	Blanch (2–3 mins), roast, or steam before freezing (9–12 months)
	Turnip	Leave in ground, protect, use as needed; or layer in damp sand (7–8 months)	Slice, blanch (2 mins), dry 55°C (8–12 hours)	Blanch (2–3 mins), roast, or mash before freezing (9–12 months)
	Celery	Leave in ground, protect, use as needed; or harvest and freeze	Slice, blanch (1 min), dry 57°C (6–8 hours)	Blanch (3 mins), portion (9–12 months)
	Celeriac	Leave in ground and use fresh	Slice, blanch (2 mins), dry 55°C (8–12 hours)	Blanch cubed (3–4 mins), roast, or mash before freezing (9–12 months)
	Fennel	Harvest and freeze; pickle, or ferment; or layer in damp sand (7–8 months)	Slice, blanch (1 min), dry 57°C (6–8 hours), bulb only	Blanch (2 mins) before freezing (8–12 months)

Kitchen Crop Masterplan

Storing Check stored produce often, and use anything showing signs of damage first.

Blanching Before freezing or drying, blanch then chill in cold water to lock in flavour and colour.

Freezing When freezing, use labelled boxes or bags and store with all labels facing the door so you can locate your produce quickly.

Dehydrating Try to keep ingredients spread in a single layer to improve air flow and speed up the process. Dehydration intensifies flavour, and you can add spice before drying. Grind dehydrated vegetables into powders for seasoning.

Pickling For pickling, see page 51 for the pickling liquor recipe. This liquor is usually used hot, but use it cold if indicated below.

Roasting and frying Use a small amount of fat (oil, butter, or lard).

Timings and temperatures Timings are a guide and will vary slightly with variety and season, but broadly, this chart covers all timings and temperatures for a wide range of cooking techniques.

Fan ovens Reduce baking or roasting temperatures by 20°C.

Pickling	Blanching	Steaming	Roasting	**Frying** (at medium or medium–high)
Yes	Cube (3–5 mins)	Small new potatoes: halve or use whole (15–20 mins)	Parboil first 200°C (40–50 mins)	Slice or dice, shallow or deep fry (5–8 mins)
Yes	Slice or dice (2–3 mins)	Slice into batons (6–10 mins)	Slice thickly 200°C (30–40 mins)	Cut into thin batons or matchsticks (5–7 mins)
Yes	Cube (2–3 mins)	Peel and cut thickly (10–15 mins)	Parboil first 200°C (35–45 mins)	Slice thinly (6–8 mins)
Yes	Cube or slice (2–3 mins)	Cube (12–15 mins)	Cube 200°C (35–45 mins)	Cut into chunks (6–8 mins)
Yes	Peel and cut into chunks or use whole baby beets (4–5 mins)	Whole (30–40 mins), skins slip off easily after	Whole or in wedges 200°C (40–60 mins)	Cut into thin slices or matchsticks (6–8 mins)
Yes	Halve or use whole if small (1 min)	Halve or use whole (5–7 mins)	Whole or halve 200°C (20–25 mins)	Slice thinly (2–3 mins)
Yes	Dice or slice (2–3 mins)	Cut into small chunks (10–12 mins)	Peel and cube 200°C (30–40 mins)	Cut into small wedges (4–6 mins)
Yes	Cut into 2–3cm pieces (2 mins)	Cut into 1–3cm chunks (5–8 mins)	Cut into chunks 190°C (25–30 mins)	Dice (3–4 mins)
Yes	Cube (2–3 mins)	Cube or slice evenly (12–15 mins)	Cut into 3–4cm wedges 200°C (35–45 mins)	Cube or slice (5–7 mins)
Yes	Slice or cut into wedges (2 mins)	Cut into wedges (8–10 mins)	Halve or slice lengthwise 190°C (30–35 mins)	Slice (5–6 mins)

	Crop	Storage	Dehydration	Freezing in portions
FRUITING VEGETABLES	Tomato	Freeze, can, chutney, pickle, dehydrate, or ferment	Slice, dry 55°C (8–12 hours)	Chop, bake, or grill, then freeze (9–12 months)
	Pepper	Freeze, pickle, dehydrate, chutney, or ferment	Slice large chillies, dry 55°C (8–12 hours)	Chop larger peppers, spread out, and freeze, then bag (9–12 months)
	Aubergine	Freeze, pickle, dehydrate, chutney, or ferment	Slice 1cm, dry 60°C (4–6 hours)	Slice and roast 200°C (20 mins), then freeze (9–12 months)
	Cucumber	Freeze, chutney, pickle, dehydrate, or ferment	Thinly slice, dry 55°C (8–10 hours)	Slice and freeze (peel and deseed first if you like) (9–12 months)
	Courgette	Freeze, can, chutney, pickle, dehydrate, or ferment	Slice, dry 55°C (8–12 hours)	Blanch (1 min) or roast 200°C (20 mins), then freeze (12 months)
	Winter Squash	Cure (10 days), then store 10–15°C, dark, ventilated (6 months)	Dice, boil (8 mins), dry 60°C (8–10 hours)	Cube and freeze raw, or roast or mash before freezing (9–12 months)
	Sweetcorn	Freeze as soon as harvested	Blanch or steam tender ears (4–6 mins), remove kernels, dry 65°C (6–10 hours)	Blanch on the cob (7–11 mins), then remove from cob, freeze in a thin layer, then bag (12 months)
ALLIUMS	Leek	Leave in ground and use fresh	Thinly chop, dry at 60°C (6–8 hours)	Clean, chop up, and blanch (1 min), then freeze (6–9 months)
	Onion	Cure (2–3 weeks) and hang somewhere cool	Peel, slice or dice, and dry 55°C (10–12 hours)	Peel, chop, and freeze (3–6 months)
	Garlic	Cure (2–4 weeks) and hang somewhere cool	Thinly slice, dry 60°C (8–10 hours)	Freeze (3–6 months)
	Spring Onion	Wash, chop, and freeze	Wash and trim the ends, cut up, dry 50°C (4–6 hours)	Clean, chop, and freeze (3–6 months)
BRASSICAS	Cabbage	Leave in ground until needed, or make kimchi (see pp.108–109)	Shred, blanch (1–2 mins), dry 55°C (10–14 hours)	Shred, blanch (2 mins), portion, and freeze (6–12 months)
	Chinese Cabbage	Refrigerate or make sauerkraut or kimchi (see pp.108–109)	Core and cut into strips, blanch (1–2 mins), dry 50°C (10–14 hours)	Shred, blanch (2 mins), portion, and freeze (6–12 months)
	Cauliflower	Portion and freeze (6–12 months)	Portion and blanch (3–4 mins), dry 60°C (10–14 hours)	Blanch 2–3 mins, portion, and freeze (6–12 months)
	Broccoli	Portion and freeze (6–12 months)	Portion and blanch (3–4 mins), dry 60°C (10–14 hours)	Blanch (2–3 mins), portion, and freeze (6–12 months)
	Brussels Sprouts	Leave in ground until needed, will last all winter	Halve and blanch (3–4 mins), dry 60°C (10–14 hours)	Halve, blanch (3–4 mins), portion, and freeze (6–12 months)
	Kale	Leave in ground over winter or wash and freeze	Remove stalks, rip leaves into pieces, dry 55°C (4–6 hours)	Wash and dry well before freezing (6–8 months)
	Pak Choi	Refrigerate or make sauerkraut or kimchi (see pp.108–109)	Separate layers, dress with oil, dry 55°C (3–4 hours)	Blanch (2 mins), portion, and freeze (6–12 months)
	Kohl Rabi	Refrigerate for 1 week or freeze (6–9 months)	Peel and slice, dry 50°C (6–10 hours)	Shred or chop, blanch (2 mins), portion, and freeze (6–12 months)

Kitchen Crop Masterplan

Pickling	Blanching	Steaming	Roasting	Frying (at medium or medium-high)
Yes (cold)	Use whole (30–60 sec), for easy peeling	–	Whole cherry best 180°C (25–30 mins)	Cut into small wedges (4–6 mins)
Yes	Slice or chop (1 min), optional before pickling	–	Chop roughly, or whole for peeling skins 200°C (10–15 mins)	Slice or whole (1–2 mins)
Yes (salt first)	Slice or chop (2–3 mins), to reduce bitterness for freezing	Cut into 2cm pieces (10–12 mins), for mashing	Halve and score flesh 200°C (30–40 mins)	Slice, salt first if needed (6–10 mins), absorbs oil
Yes	–	–	–	–
Yes	Slice (1–2 mins), for freezing	Cut into thick rounds (5–7 mins)	Slice thickly 200°C (20–25 mins)	Cut into thin coins or batons (3–5 mins)
Yes	Peel and cube (2–3 mins), for freezing	Cube (15–20 mins) until fork-tender	Halve or cut into wedges 200°C (40–50 mins)	Dice or grate into fritters (8–10 mins)
Yes (blanched)	Whole cob or kernels (4–6 mins), then ice bath	Whole on cob for juicy sweetness (10–15 mins)	Whole on cob 200°C (25–30 mins)	Kernels or fritters (3–5 mins)
Yes	Cut into rounds or splits (2–3 mins)	Halve lengthways (8–10 mins)	Halve or slice 190°C (25–30 mins)	Slice (5–6 mins)
Yes	Whole or cut into wedges (2–3 mins)	Whole small onions (10–15 mins)	Cut into wedges or use whole small onions 200°C (35–45 mins)	Chop or slice (8–10 mins)
Yes	Whole cloves (1 min)	–	Whole bulbs in foil 180°C (30–40 mins)	Slice thinly or crush (1–2 mins), don't burn
Yes	Whole or chopped (1–2 mins)	Whole (4 mins) or chop (1–2 mins)	Whole or in large chunks 200°C (15–20 mins)	Slice finely or up to 1cm (2–3 mins)
Yes	Leaves or quarters (2–3 mins)	Shred or cut into wedges (6–8 mins)	Cut into wedges 200°C (25–30 mins)	Shred (3–5 mins)
Yes	Leafy portions (1–2 mins)	Halve or quarter (6–8 mins) or shred (3–4 mins)	–	Shred (2–3 mins)
Yes	Florets (3–4 mins)	Florets (6–10 mins)	Florets or cut into steaks 200°C (25–35 mins)	Florets or cut into steaks, shallow or deep fry (6–8 mins)
Yes	Florets or tender stems (2–3 mins)	Florets (5–7 mins)	Florets 200°C (15–20 mins)	Small florets or stems (5–7 mins)
Yes	Whole, but cross-score base first (3–5 mins)	Halve (7–10 mins)	Halve, cut-side down 200°C (25–30 mins)	Halve (5–8 mins), cut-side down
Yes	Destem leaves (1–2 mins)	Remove thick stems (5–6 mins)	Leaves, for kale crisps 180°C (10–15 mins)	Crisp leaves (2–3 mins)
Yes	Stems then leaves (1–2 mins)	Halve or use whole (4–5 mins)	–	Stems then leaves (2–4 mins)
Yes	Slice or dice (2–3 mins)	Slice or cut into chunks (8–10 mins)	Peel and cut 200°C (30–40 mins)	Slice or grate (4–6 mins)

	Crop	Storage	Dehydration	Freezing in portions
LEGUMES	Peas	Pod and freeze as soon as they're harvested	Pod and blanch (2 mins), dry 60°C (6–10 hours)	Pod and blanch (1 min), then freeze (6–9 months)
	Climbing Beans	Pick (pod), dry on a windowsill in sun; store in an airtight container	Pod and blanch (3 mins), dry 60°C (6–10 hours)	Blanch (2–3 mins) and freeze (6–9 months)
	Dwarf Beans	Pick and refrigerate (7 days) or freeze	Blanch (2 mins), dry 60°C (6–10 hours)	Blanch (1–2 mins) and freeze (6–9 months)
	Fava Beans	Pick (pod), dry on a windowsill in sun; store in an airtight container	Pod and blanch (2 mins), dry 60°C (6–10 hours)	Blanch (3 mins) and freeze (6–9 months)
LEAFY GREENS	Chard	Blanch and freeze, or blend into a pesto (see p.169)	Remove stalks, dry 55°C (4–6 hours)	Blanch (2 mins) and freeze (6–9 months)
	Lettuce	Refrigerate after harvest and keep dry (4–5 days)	Dry 35°C (6–10 hours), grind into powder, condition 50°C (20 mins)	–
	Spinach	Refrigerate after harvest and keep dry (5 days)	Dry 55°C (4–6 hours)	Blanch (2 mins) and freeze (6–9 months)
	Chicory	Leave in ground until needed, then refrigerate (5–7 days)	Young tender leaves: dry 35–45°C (4–8 hours)	Blanch (2 mins) and freeze (6–9 months)
	Endive	Refrigerate after harvest and keep dry (7 days)	–	Blanch (2 mins) and freeze (6–9 months)
	Rocket	Refrigerate after harvest and keep dry (7 days), make a pesto	Dry 35–45°C (4–8 hours), grind into coarse powder	Blanch (2 mins) and freeze (6–9 months)
	Mustard	Refrigerate after harvest and keep dry (7 days), make a pesto	Dry 35–45°C (3–5 hours)	Blanch (2 mins) and freeze (6–9 months)
HERBS	Coriander	Dry seeds on windowsill, use leaves for pesto, compound butter	Dry 35–45°C (3–5 hours)	Freeze chopped in water or oil in ice cube trays
	Basil	Make pesto or dehydrate	Pick just before drying and avoid washing, dry 35–45°C (4–6 hours)	Chop, blend with olive oil and freeze as cubes
	Parsley	Dry seeds on windowsill, make pesto, or dehydrate	Dry 35–45°C (4–6 hours)	Chop and freeze flat in bags or in oil cubes
	Dill	Dry seeds on windowsill, make pesto, or dehydrate	Dry 35–45°C (2–4 hours)	Chop finely and freeze in water or as sprigs in a freezer bag
	Thyme	Harvest as needed (grows all year)	Pick when flowering, dry 35–45°C (2–4 hours)	Freeze whole sprigs in bags or chop and cube in oil
	Rosemary	Harvest as needed (grows all year)	Dry 35–45°C (4–6 hours), strip leaves after drying	Freeze sprigs directly, strip leaves as needed
	Sage	Make pesto, compound butter, herb oil, or dehydrate	Dry 35–45°C (4–6 hours), flip halfway to prevent curling	Freeze whole leaves flat on a tray, then bag
	Oregano	Make pesto, compound butter, herb oil, or dehydrate	Dry 35–45°C (3–5 hours) on the stem, then crumble and sieve out any woody bits	Freeze as whole sprigs or chopped in oil
	Chives	Make pesto, compound butter, herb oil, vinegar infusion or dehydrate	Dry 35–45°C (2–3 hours)	Chop and freeze flat in bags

Pickling	Blanching	Steaming	Roasting	Frying (at medium or medium–high)
Yes	Shell or pod first (1–2 mins)	Shell first (3–5 mins) until just tender	–	Whole (2–3 mins)
Yes	Slice or use whole (2–3 mins)	Trim ends, whole (5–7 mins)	Whole 190°C (15–20 mins)	Slice or whole (3–4 mins)
Yes	Slice or use whole (2–3 mins)	Whole (5–6 mins)	Whole 190°C (15–20 mins)	Slice or whole (3–4 mins)
Yes	Pod first (2–3 mins), for easy double-podding	Pod first (5–7 mins), double-podding optional	Peel young beans 190°C (20–25 mins)	Double pod then sauté (3–5 mins)
Yes	Stems first, then leaves (1–2 mins)	Stems first, then leaves (3–5 mins)	Leaves, for crisps 190°C (10–15 mins)	Stems first, then leaves (3–5 mins)
Yes (cold)	–	Leaves (2–3 mins), for firmer varieties	–	Halve (1–2 mins), cut-side down, firm varieties best
Yes	Leaves (30–60 sec)	Leaves (2–3 mins), until just wilted	–	Leaves (2–3 mins), wilts quickly
Yes	Leaves (1–2 mins), for freezing or grilling	Halve (6–8 mins)	Halve 200°C (20–25 mins)	Halve (4–5 mins), cut-side down
Yes	Leaves (1–2 mins), for freezing or grilling	Halve (6–8 mins)	Halve 200°C (20–25 mins)	Halve (4–5 mins), cut-side down
Yes	Leaves (30 sec)	–	–	Leaves (1 min), flash fry
Yes	Leaves (1–2 mins)	Leaves (4–6 mins)	–	Leaves (2–3 mins)
Yes	Leaves (10 sec), for vibrant green sauces	–	–	–
Yes	Leaves (10 sec), to keep colour in pesto	–	–	Leaves (10–20 sec), flash fry
Yes	Leaves (10 sec), to brighten colour and make less bitter	–	–	Leaves (10–20 sec), flash fry for garnish
Yes	Leaves (10–15 sec), optional for freezing	–	–	–
Yes	–	–	Sprinkle on roasts at end 200°C (2–3 mins)	Whole sprigs (1–2 mins), to flavour oil
Yes	–	–	Add to roasts near end 200°C (2–3 mins)	Whole sprigs (1–2 mins), to infuse oil
Yes	–	–	Leaves 200°C (2–3 mins)	Crisp leaves (20–30 sec), for garnish
Yes	–	–	Whole sprigs 200°C (2–3 mins)	–
Yes	Leaves (10–15 sec), optional for freezing	–	–	–

	Crop	Storage	Dehydration	Freezing in portions
HERBS	Mint	Dehydrate or oxidize first	Dry 35–45°C (2–4 hours)	Freeze leaves in ice cubes (water or tea)
	Lemon Verbena	Oxidize and dehydrate	Dry 35–45°C (2–4 hours), whole if possible	Freeze in tea or syrup form
	Lemon Balm	Dehydrate or oxidize first	Dry 35–45°C (2–3 hours), crush gently before infusing	Freeze leaves in ice cubes (water or tea)
	Lavender	Hang and dry	Dry 35–45°C (2–4 hours), buds should remain purple	Freeze flowers in sugar or infuse in syrup
	Korean Mint	Oxidize and dehydrate	Whole sprigs, dry 35–45°C (2–4 hours), then strip leaves and flowers	Freeze leaves in cubes (tea or oil)
SOFT FRUIT	Strawberry	Make into jams, jellies, curd; freeze or dehydrate	Dry 55–60°C (12–18 hours)	Hull, slice, freeze flat, then bag
	Raspberry	Make into jams, jellies, curd; freeze or dehydrate	Dry 50–55°C (12–18 hours)	Freeze whole on tray
	Blackberry	Make into jams, jellies, curd; freeze or dehydrate	Cut large berries in half, cut-side up, dry 50–55°C (12–18 hours)	Freeze whole on tray
	Blueberry	Make into jams, jellies, curd; freeze or dehydrate	Pierce with a needle or blanch briefly, dry 50–55°C (16–24 hours)	Freeze whole, unwashed
	Gooseberry	Make into jams, jellies, curd; freeze or dehydrate	Slice in half for quicker drying, dry 50–55°C (10–16 hours)	Top and tail first, freeze whole
	Blackcurrant	Make into jams, jellies, curd; freeze or dehydrate	Dry 50–55°C (14–20 hours)	Freeze whole
	Redcurrant	Make into jams, jellies, curd; freeze or dehydrate	Dry 50–55°C (12–18 hours), on the stalk if small	Freeze on stems or strip and freeze in trays
	Rhubarb	Make into jams, jellies, curd; freeze or dehydrate	Slice thin (5mm) or julienne, dry 55–60°C (8–12 hours)	Slice into 2.5cm chunks, freeze on trays, then bag
EDIBLE FLOWERS	Nasturtium	Infuse flowers in vinegar, leaves for pesto, pickle flowers and seeds	Whole flowers or petals flat, dry 35–40°C (2–4 hours)	Freeze flowers in ice cubes
	Rose	Oxidize young leaves, infuse petals in white vinegar	Remove petals from the base, dry 35–40°C (2–6 hours)	–
	Cosmos	Dehydrate petals	Dry 35–40°C (2–6 hours)	–
	Calendula	Dehydrate petals	Petals only, dry 35–40°C (2–4 hours)	–
	Borage	Infuse flowers in white vinegar, freeze them in ice for drinks	Petals or flowers on mesh or paper, dry 35°C (2–3 hours)	Freeze in ice cubes
	Zinnia	Dehydrate petals	Dry 35–40°C (2–4 hours), more decorative than tasty	–

Kitchen Crop Masterplan

Pickling	Blanching	Steaming	Roasting	Frying (at medium or medium–high
Yes	Leaves (10–15 sec), for freezing for infusions	–	–	–
Yes	Leaves (10–15 sec), to keep fragrance for freezing	–	–	–
Yes	Leaves (10–15 sec), for colour retention	–	–	–
Yes	–	–	–	–
Yes	Leaves (10–15 sec), for freezing	–	–	–
Yes (cold)	–	–	–	Halve (1–2 mins)
Yes (cold)	–	–	–	–
Yes (cold)	–	–	–	Whole (1–2 mins), in butter
Yes (cold)	–	–	Whole, in bakes 190°C (10–15 mins)	Whole (1–2 mins)
Yes (cold)	Whole (30–60 sec), for jam or sauce base	Whole for jams (3–4 mins)	Top and tailed, in glazes 190°C (15–20 mins),	Whole (2–3 mins)
Yes (cold)	Whole (30–60 sec), optional before preserving	–	Whole, in bakes 190°C (10–15 mins)	Whole (1–2 mins), gently
Yes (cold)	–	–	On stems 190°C (10–15 mins)	–
Yes (cold)	Slice (1–2 mins), for freezing or compotes	Cut into short batons (5–7 mins), check for softness	Cut into batons, check often 190°C (15–20 mins)	Cube (3–5 mins)
Yes	–	–	–	Flash fry flowers or leaves (10–20 sec)
Yes (cold)	–	–	–	–
Yes	–	–	–	–
Yes (cold)	–	–	–	Petals (10–20 sec), crisp as garnish
Yes (cold)	–	–	–	–
Yes (cold)	–	–	–	–

Resources

GROWING RESOURCES

Seeds and Plants
Real Seeds realseeds.co.uk
Wales Seed Hub seedhub.wales
Kings Seeds kingsseeds.com
David Austin Roses davidaustinroses.co.uk

Compost, Feed, and Mulch
Melcourt melcourt.co.uk (peat-free compost)
Dalefoot dalefoot.co.uk (peat-free compost)
Câr-y-môr carymor.wales (seaweed feed)
Eco Crops ecocrops.co.uk (woodchip mulch)

Tools
Gardena gardena.com/uk
Garland Products garlandproducts.com

Recycled Plant Labels
The Essentials Company
theessentialscompany.co.uk

Polytunnels
First Tunnels firsttunnels.co.uk

Heated Propagation and Lighting
Simply Seed simplyseed.co.uk
Harrod Horticultural harrodhorticultural.com

Books
The Self-Sufficiency Garden Huw Richards and Sam Cooper
The Vegetable Grower's Handbook Huw Richards
Allotment Month By Month Alan Buckingham
Nettles & Petals Jamie Walton

Recommended YouTube Channels
Charles Dowding
Grow Veg
Liz Zorab

Frost Dates Map and Growing Zones
plantmaps.com

KITCHEN RESOURCES

Essential Ingredients
Sous Chef (pantry staples & specialist salts) souschef.co.uk
Seasoned Pioneers (spices & blends) seasonedpioneers.com
Belazu (vinegars, oils, preserved lemons) belazu.com

Equipment
Taski (quality Japanese knives) taski.store
Kilner (jars) kilnerjar.co.uk
Kitchen Provisions (quality knives & Japanese tools) kitchenprovisions.co.uk
Thermapen (temperature accuracy for preserving & cooking) thermapen.co.uk

Books
The Fermentation Kitchen Sam Cooper
Salt, Fat, Acid, Heat Samin Nosrat
The Science of Fermentation Robin Sherriff
The River Cottage Preserves Handbook Pam Corbin
Six Seasons: A New Way with Vegetables Joshua McFadden
Sift Nicola Lamb

Further Learning
Oxford Symposium on Food & Cookery oxfordsymposium.org.uk
Slow Food UK slowfood.org.uk
The Black Butter Club Sam Cooper's seasonal food newsletter

Index

A
agastache 161
air-frying 27
allium 86–101, 200
aloo palak 145
annual herbs 20, 21, 152–5
aphids 136, 205
apple 120, 123
aubergine 78–9
　cooking 73, 79, 148
　growing 78
　miso aubergine, green beans and barley 73

B
baking 26
　see also salt, salt-baking
banana, cooking with 120
barbecuing 27
basil 154, 162–3, 166–7
　basil pesto 169
bay 29, 53, 94, 162, 203
beans
　French 130–1
　green 73
　haricot 55, 59
　tinned, dried & jarred 23
　see also butter beans; climbing beans; dwarf beans; fava beans; runner beans
beds 12–13
　in-ground 12
　raised 12, 20
beetroot 46–9
　cooking 48–9, 120, 123
　growing 46–7
　quick mixed beetroot salad 49
　slow-roasted beetroot salad 48–9
blackberry 178–81
　blackberry gin 180–1
　growing 178–81

blackbirds 172, 179, 183, 191, 194
blackcurrant 190–3
　blackcurrant boshi 192–3
　blackcurrant glaze 85
　growing 190–1
blackfly 136
blanching 26, 58
blossom end rot 65, 69, 72, 79
blueberries 182–5
　blueberry coulis 184–5
　cheesecake 184–5
　growing 182–3
boiling 25
bolting 50, 58, 140, 142, 144, 148–9, 152–3
borage 207
boshi, blackcurrant 192–3
braising 26
brassicas 102–23, 202
broad beans see fava beans
broccoli 112–15
　broccoli and sheep's curd tart 114–15
　calabrese 112–13
　growing 112–13
　sprouting 112–13
Brussels sprouts 116–17
　growing 116
　sautéed sprouts with chestnuts 117
bulgur 23
buns, grilled potato 35–6
burgers, courgette and lentil 80–1
butter, herb compound 164
butter beans 55
　baked beans 67
　baked celeriac 57
　braised leeks and butter beans 90–1

C
cabbage 104–6
　cooking 106, 123
　growing 104–5
　okonomiyaki 106
cabbage white caterpillars 44, 105, 110, 113, 119, 202
calendula (pot marigold) 200, 206
cape gooseberry 187
capers, nasturtium 203
capsicum 68
caramelization 26, 27
carbs 23
carpaccio, courgette 80
carrot 20, 38–41
　carrot miso hummus 40–1
　cooking 40–1, 53, 55, 67, 120, 123
　growing 38–9
carrot root fly 39
casserole, braised fennel and haricot 59
caterpillars 44, 105, 110, 113, 119, 187, 202
cauliflower 110–11
　cauliflower gratin 111
celeriac 56–7
　baked celeriac 57
celery 53, 54–5
　celery and Stilton soup 55
chard 140–1
　cooking 120, 141
　growing 140
　stir-fried noodles with chard 141
charring 28
cheese 23, 173
　baked celeriac 57
　basil pesto 169
　cauliflower gratin 111
　celery and Stilton soup 55

endive and pear winter salad 147
French onion soup 94–5
garden pea and Korean mint risotto 128–9
rocket crêpes 148
spring onion fritters 101
swede tartiflette 45
see also goat's cheese
cheesecake 184–5
chervil 163
chestnuts with sautéed sprouts 117
chicken 169, 173
chickpea(s) 38
chicory 146
  pan-fried 146
chillies 8, 68–71, 166
Chinese cabbage 107–9
  growing 107
  kimchi 108–9
chives 123, 159, 200
  chive and oat crackers 168
chutney, rhubarb 197
citrus 22
  lemon and tahini dressing 143
clafoutis, raspberry 176–7
climbing beans 130–3, 142
  charred runner beans and trout 132–3
  growing 130–1
comfrey 13
companion planting 202, 206
compost 8–9, 12–15
compost bins 14, 15
confit 27
container growing 8, 13
  see also specific crops
cooking techniques
  dry heat 26
  specialized 27–8
  for vegetables 25–7
  water-based 25–6
  see also specific crops
coriander 21, 154, 162–3, 166
  herb salt 166
cornflower petals 120
cosmos, sulphur 206
coulis, blueberry 184–5

courgette 11, 78–81
  courgette carpaccio 80
  courgette and lentil burger 80–1
  flowers 200
  growing 78–9
crackers, chive and oat 168
crêpes, rocket 148
croutons 94–5
cucumber 74–7
  growing 74–5
  quick pickled cucumber salad 76
  sunomono salad 77
curd, gooseberry 188–9

D
damping off 68
damsons 180
dandelion 13
deep-frying 27
dehydrating 28
dill 155, 162–3, 166
division 196
docks 13
dressings 147, 149, 169
  lemon and tahini 143
dwarf beans 18, 134–5
  growing 134
  tempura 135

E
edible flowers 99, 198–207
eggs 114–15
  cheesecake 184–5
  gooseberry curd 188–9
  raspberry clafoutis 176–7
  tortilla 37
elderberries 180
endive 147
  endive and pear winter salad 147
equipment 8–9

F
falafel, broad bean 137
farro 23
fava beans 136–7
  broad bean falafel 137
  growing 136

feeding plants 12–13
  see also specific crops
fennel 58–9
  braised fennel and haricot casserole 59
  growing 58
fermenting 28
fertility needs 12–13
feta
  rocket crêpes 148
  spring onion fritters 101
fish 43, 169
  charred runner beans and trout 132–3
  fisherman's stew 67
  tinned oily 23
flea beetles 44, 51, 52
fleece 11
flours 23
flowers see edible flowers
French beans 130–1
French marjoram 158
fritters, spring onion 101
frost protection 11
fruit see soft fruit; specific fruit
fruit cages 175
fruit rot 79, 82
fruiting vegetables 60–85

G
galette, winter squash and goat's cheese 83
gaps, plugging 21
garlic 96–9
  cured 99
  flowers 99
  green 98
  growing 96–7
  scapes 99
  tops 99
  wet 98
gin
  blackberry 180–1
  rose-infused 205
goat's cheese
  mustard leaf salad 149
  winter squash and goat's cheese galette 83

Index

gooseberry 186–9
   gooseberry curd 188–9
   growing 186–7
gooseberry sawfly 187
gratin, cauliflower 111
green beans
   miso aubergine, green beans and barley 73
greenhouses, mini 9
grilling 27
growing cages/domes 127
growing techniques 10–11
   see also specific crops

H
hardening off 11
haricot beans 55
   braised fennel and haricot casserole 59
herbs 150–69
   annual 20, 21, 152–5
   basil pesto 169
   chive and oat crackers 168
   cooking with 120, 123, 162–9
   dried 163
   fresh 162–7
   growing 152–5, 156–61
   hard 162, 163
   herb compound butter 164
   herb oil 165
   herb salt 166
   herb sugar 166
   herbal teas 167, 177
   perennial 156–61
   pickling 165
   rosemary and olive scones 168
   soft 162–3
hot sauce 70
hummus, carrot miso 40–1

I
insects 18, 20, 42, 140, 201
islands 20

J
jam
   setting 28
   strawberry 173
Japanese wineberries 179
jars, sterilizing 28
jelly, redcurrant 195

K
kale 11, 20–1, 118–21
   growing 119–10
   kale smoothie 120–1
   perennial 119
kimchi 108–9
kitchen staples 22–3
kitchen techniques 24–9
knife skills 24–5
kohl rabi 123
   growing 123
   kohl rabi slaw 123
Korean mint 161
   garden pea and Korean mint risotto 128–9

L
labels 9
Lancashire hotpot 37
lavender 161, 166–7
   herb sugar 166
layers 20
leaf miners 89, 140, 144
leafy greens 138–49
leek 11, 88–91
   braised leeks and butter beans 90–1
   cooking 59, 90–1, 114–15
   growing 88–9
leek moth (onion leaf miner) 89
legumes 124–37
lemon balm 156, 160, 163, 166–7
lemon and tahini dressing 143
lemon verbena 120, 156, 160, 163, 166–7
   oxidized lemon verbena tea 167
lentil(s) 53, 169
   courgette and lentil burger 80–1
   tinned, dried, jarred 23
lettuce 20, 142–3
   charred lettuce with lemon and tahini dressing 143
   growing 142
light 8
loganberries 179

M
Maillard reaction 26
mangetout 126–7
marjoram 162, 163
   see also French marjoram
mice 84, 134, 136
microclimates 18
microgreens 38
microwaving 28
mildew, powdery 75, 79, 82
mint 120, 156, 159, 166–7
miso 22, 49, 55, 108
   carrot miso hummus 40–1
   miso aubergine, green beans and barley 73
monocultures 18
mulching 11
   see also specific crops
mushroom
   courgette and lentil burger 80–1
   dried 23
   stir-fried noodles with chard 141
   vegetable turnip hotpot 53
mustard 149
mustard leaf salad 149

N
nasturtium 18, 202–3
   capers 203
   growing 202
nature-inspired design 18
nematodes 107
netting 105, 113, 194
nettles 13
noodles, stir-fried noodles with chard 141
nourishment 6
nutritional yeast 23

O
oat and chive crackers 168
oils 22
   herb 165
okonomiyaki 106
olive and rosemary scones 168
onion 18–20, 92–5
   cooking 59, 67, 94–5, 148
   French onion soup 94–5
   growing 92–3
   sets 92
onion flies 93, 100

onion leaf miner 93
oregano 123, 158, 162, 200

P
pak choi 122
pan-frying 27
parsley 120, 155, 162–3, 166
parsnip 42–3
   cooking 43, 45
   growing 42
   parsnip purée 43
parsnip canker 42
pasta 23
   arrabiata 67
pastry, shortcrust 114–15
pear 120
   endive and pear winter salad 147
pearl barley 23
   miso aubergine, green beans and barley 73
peas 126–9
   garden pea and Korean mint risotto 128–9
   growing 126–7
pepper 10, 68–71
   cooking 70–1, 148
   growing 68–9
   hot sauce 70–1
peppercorns 22
perennial herbs 156–61
pesto, basil 169
pests 18, 39
   see also specific pests
pickles
   pickled radish 51
   pickling herbs 165
   pickling technique 28
   quick pickled cucumber salad 76
pigeons 105, 110, 113, 119, 127
pizza 67
poaching 26
polenta 23
polyculture 18, 200
polytunnels 9, 62–4, 68, 72, 74, 78, 82, 100, 134, 160, 187
potato blight 34
potato scab 34

potatoes 16, 18–20, 32–7
   aloo palak 145
   chitting 32
   cooking 35–7, 45, 55, 145, 169
   grilled potato buns 35–6
   growing 32–4
   Lancashire hotpot 37
   maincrop 32, 33
   new 34, 35
   tortilla 37
potting on 10
presence 6
preserving 27–8
protein, preserved 23
pruning
   cucumber 75
   roses 204
   soft fruit 172, 174–5, 178–9, 183, 186, 190, 194
purée, parsnip 43
push–pull technique 39, 42

R
radish 50–1
   cooking 51, 76
   growing 50–1
   pickled radish 51
   winter 50
raspberry 174–7
   autumn-fruiting 175
   growing 174–5
   raspberry clafoutis 176–7
   summer-fruiting 174–5
raspberry leaf tea 167, 177
redcurrant 194–5
   growing 194
   redcurrant jelly 195
refinement 6
rhubarb 196–7
   chutney 197
   growing 196
   juice 197
   roasted 197
rice 23, 128–9, 193
risotto, garden pea and Korean mint 128–9
roasting 26, 48–9, 169, 197

rocket 148
   cooking with 57, 148
   rocket crêpes 148
rodents 47, 84, 127, 134, 136
root vegetables 31–59, 120
   storing in sand 47
rose 120, 167, 204–5
   salt 205
   syrup 205
rose hips 205
rosemary 156–7, 162–3, 166–7, 200
   rosemary and olive scones 168
runner beans 130–1, 200
   charred runner beans and trout 132–3
rust 89, 97

S
sage 123, 158, 162, 166–7
salads
   endive and pear winter 147
   mustard leaf 149
   quick mixed beetroot 49
   quick pickled cucumber 76
   sunomono 77
salt 22
   herb 166
   rose 205
salt-baking 28
sandwiches 169
sauces 28
   hot sauce 70–1
   kitchen staples 22
   pan sauces 28
sautéing 27
savory 163
scapes 99
scones, rosemary and olive 168
searing 27
seaweed
   fertilizer 13
   sunomono salad 77
seedlings 11
   see also specific crops
seeds 8, 10
   see also specific crops
self-sufficiency formula 16–17
setting jams 28

Index

sheep's curd and broccoli and tart 114–15
simmering 26
slaw, kohl rabi 123
slow-cooking 26
slug nematodes 107
slugs 105, 107, 119, 131, 134, 142, 172, 196
smoking 27
smoothies, kale 120–1
soft fruit 170–97
soup 43, 169, 193
   celery and Stilton 55
   French onion 94–5
sous vide 28
soy sauce 22
spinach 144–5
   aloo palak 145
   cooking 120, 145
   growing 144
spring onion 100–1
   cooking 101, 123
   growing 100
   spring onion fritters 101
squash 11, 45
staking plants 118
steaming 26
sterilizing jars 28
stew, fisherman's 67
stewing 26
stir-frying 27
   stir-fried noodles with chard 141
stocks 29
strawberry 172–3
   cooking 120, 173
   growing 172
   strawberry jam 173
sugar, herb 166
sugarsnap peas 126–7
sulphur cosmos 206
supporting plants 64, 74–5, 118, 126–7, 130–1, 134, 172
   "boxing rings" 126–7
sweating 27
swede 44–5
   growing 444
   swede tartiflette 45

sweetcorn 18, 84–5, 142
   barbecued sweetcorn with blackcurrant 85
   growing 84
sylvanberries 179
syrup, rose 205

T
tahini 38
   lemon and tahini dressing 143
tamari sauce 22
tarragon 163, 166
tarts 43
   broccoli and sheep's curd 114–15
tayberry 179
teas, herbal 167, 177
tempura dwarf beans 135
thistles 13
thyme 156–7, 162–3, 166–7, 180, 200
tomato blight 65
tomatoes 9, 10, 62–7
   cooking 53, 66–7, 70
   cordon 68
   determinate (bush) 62, 64, 65
   growing 62–5
   indeterminate (cordon) 62, 64–5
   pinching out 64, 65
   skin-on tomato sauce 66–7
   supporting 64
tools 9
tortilla 37
transplanting 11
trays 8
trout and charred runner beans 132–3
turnip 52–3
   growing 52
   vegetable turnip hotpot 53

V
vegetables 6–21, 31–169
   allium 86–101, 200
   brassicas 102–23, 202
   compost for 14–15
   fruiting vegetables 60–85
   growing essentials 8–13

herbs 150–69
leafy greens 138–49
legumes 124–37
and polyculture 18–21
roast vegetables 169
root vegetables 31–59, 120
and the self-sufficiency formula 16–17
see also specific vegetables
vinegars 22, 28, 48–9, 51, 76–7, 128, 141, 143, 146–7, 149, 162, 165, 173, 176, 200, 203
voles 47, 84, 134, 136

W
watering 10–11
see also specific crops
wind damage 113
winter squash 82–3
   growing 82
   winter squash and goat's cheese galette 83
Worcestershire sauce 22

Z
zero-waste crops 47
zinnia 207

Acknowledgments

HUW RICHARDS
This book has been made possible by the incredible team of friends, family, and colleagues I have around me. First and foremost to Sam, my fellow author, friend, and colleague who has inspired me more than he knows when it comes to ingredients, flavour, and pushing the limits of what is possible both in the garden and the kitchen. He's made me a true kitchen gardener!

Our colleagues Eleri, Will, and Llyr have also been a wonderful support, taking on additional jobs and responsibilities to help make sure I had enough time to give this book the attention it deserves.

Away from the garden, my DK "family" have been nothing short of brilliant, especially when patiently waiting for my text to arrive when Sam had completed his months before! To Ruth, Lucy, Jordan, Christine, Jane, and my publisher Stephanie – a heartfelt thank you for enabling these ideas and dreams to become reality.

SAM COOPER
In no particular order, I would like to thank Ruth O'Rourke, Jordan Lambley, and Lucy Philpott, our ever-patient winning team at DK. And of course Jane Simmonds, our copy editor, who turned our scribbles and notes into a book to be proud of.

I would also like to thank my wife, Wai Yan, who gladly ate everything I cooked for this book – even the celeriac – and remembered to sow carrots when the rest of us forgot. To my friends and family, who each, in their own small way, inspire me daily. And of course Huw, and our weird and wonderful team – Llyr, Eleri, and Will – where would I be without them?

Thank you to Ultracomida for teaching me to make the best tortilla I've ever eaten.

Lastly, I would like to dedicate a special thanks to the incredible community who have found me online. You are a collective creative force to be reckoned with. Gardeners, farmers, foragers, cooks, chefs, fermenters, and everyone in between: thank you.

About the Authors

Huw Richards is a permaculturalist and digital creator based in midwest Wales. At age 12, he discovered permaculture and created his own YouTube channel (@HuwRichards) about growing your own food. He now has more than 900,000 YouTube subscribers, and his videos have collectively been viewed more than 100 million times on YouTube and Instagram (@huwsgarden). Huw shares his growing know-how via his videos and substack (huwrichards.substack.com), as well as in his books: *Veg in One Bed*, *Grow Food for Free*, *The Vegetable Grower's Handbook*, *The Self-Sufficiency Garden*, and *The Permaculture Garden*.

Sam Cooper is a chef, fermenter, photographer, illustrator, and gardener. He began working in kitchens before meeting Huw Richards and joining the team at the farm in mid-west Wales. Since then, he has garnered a following of almost 600,000 as @chef.sam.black on Instagram, where he shares videos using homegrown, seasonal, and foraged produce. He also writes about all things food on his substack The Black Butter Club (chefsamblack.substack.com). Sam wrote the In the Kitchen chapter of *The Self-Sufficiency Garden* (co-authored with Huw Richards), as well as two books of his own: *The Fermentation Kitchen* and *The Nature of Food*.

PUBLISHER'S ACKNOWLEDGMENTS

DK would like to thank Kathryn Glendenning and Alice Groser for proofreading, Lisa Footitt for indexing, Jason Ingram for the photograph of lavender (p161), and Matt Cox at Newman+Eastwood Ltd for the design concept.

PICTURE CREDITS

The publisher would also like to thank the following for their kind permission to reproduce their photographs:

100 GAP Photos: Martin Hughes-Jones. **112 Alamy Stock Photo**: Skye Hohmann. **186 Alamy Stock Photo:** Karen Parker Photography.

DK LONDON
Editorial Director Ruth O'Rourke
Project Editor Lucy Philpott
Senior Designer Jordan Lambley
Production Editor Robert Dunn
Production Controller Kariss Ainsworth
DTP and Design Coordinator Heather Blagden
Jacket and Sales Material Coordinator Serena Sclocco
Art Director Maxine Pedliham
Publishing Director Stephanie Jackson

Editorial Jane Simmonds
Design Christine Keilty
Photography Huw Richards and Sam Cooper
Jacket Illustrations Sam Cooper

First published in Great Britain in 2026 by
Dorling Kindersley Limited
20 Vauxhall Bridge Road,
London SW1V 2SA

The authorised representative in the EEA is
Dorling Kindersley Verlag GmbH. Arnulfstr. 124,
80636 Munich, Germany

Text and photography copyright © Huw Richards 2026
Huw Richards has asserted his right to be identified as the author of this work.
Copyright © 2026 Dorling Kindersley Limited
A Penguin Random House Company
10 9 8 7 6 5 4 3 2 1
001– 351978–Mar/2026

All rights reserved.
No part of this publication may be reproduced, stored in or introduced into a retrieval system, or transmitted, in any form, or by any means (electronic, mechanical, photocopying, recording, or otherwise), without the prior written permission of the copyright owner.
No part of this publication may be used or reproduced in any manner for the purpose of training artificial intelligence technologies or systems. In accordance with Article 4(3) of the DSM Directive 2019/790, DK expressly reserves this work from the text and data mining exception.

A CIP catalogue record for this book
is available from the British Library.
ISBN: 978-0-2417-6703-0

Printed and bound in Italy

www.dk.com

This book was made with Forest Stewardship Council™ certified paper – one small step in DK's commitment to a sustainable future. Learn more at www.dk.com/uk/information/sustainability